WARWICKSHIRE
COLLEGE
LIBRARY

796.019
O'CO
(D23)

NLP & SPORTS

WITHDRAWN

D0313879

WARWICKSHIRE
COLLEGE
LIBRARY

NLP &
SPORTS

*How to Win the
Mind Game*

JOSEPH O'CONNOR

Thorsons

Warwickshire College
Library
Moreton Morrell Centre

Class No: 796.019

Acc No: 00519886

Thorsons
An Imprint of HarperCollins*Publishers*
77–85 Fulham Palace Road
Hammersmith, London W6 8JB

The Thorsons website address is: www.thorsons.com

Published by Thorsons 2001

10 9 8 7 6 5 4 3 2 1

© Joseph O'Connor 2001

Joseph O'Connor asserts the moral right to
be identified as the author of this work

A catalogue record for this book
is available from the British Library

ISBN 0 7225 3671 2

Illustrations by Peter Cox Associates

Printed and bound in Great Britain by
Creative Print and Design Wales, Ebbw Vale

All rights reserved. No part of this publication may be
reproduced, stored in a retrieval system, or transmitted,
in any form or by any means, electronic, mechanical,
photocopying, recording or otherwise, without the prior
permission of the publishers.

Contents

Acknowledgements

First I would like to acknowledge John Grinder and Richard Bandler, the co-developers of NLP, also Robert Dilts, whose work and research have added much to the field.

My thanks to all the athletes who took the time to help me with the book, especially Alex Couch, Jamie Delgado, Roger Winchester and John Sewell. Thanks to Ron Banks for sharing his work on unconscious process in peak performance.

Thank you again to Carole Tonkinson, my editor at Thorsons, for her unfailing support and also to Elizabeth Hutchins for her work on the manuscript.

John Prine, Sarah McLachlan, Oasis and Smashmouth provided the music I enjoyed during the time I was writing this book.

Introduction

When you play sport you express yourself in a unique way. You combine the sheer joy of physical movement with the mental skills of strategy, tactics and the extra edge of competing with others. Sport engages your emotions not only when you play, but also when you watch. You care, sometimes passionately, identify with 'your' teams and players; sports programmes on television have large audiences; the biggest city arenas are sports arenas. Sport is a different world from the world of work (although competition enters into both!), one in which you use different skills and can excel in a completely different way. There is probably only one other human activity that gives more pleasure to more people than sport.

You are involved and interested in sport, or you would not be reading this book, and I assume you want to become more skilful and enjoy it more, whatever level you compete at. You will remember with pleasure the times you played well – when you were in the 'flow state' or 'in the zone'. Do you want to take the magic ingredient from those times and use it to play like that more often? You will also no doubt remember the times you played badly – you were in 'the pits'. Do you want to learn from those so they never happen again? This book will help you to achieve both these goals.

Physical skill is important in sport, but bodies do not compete, people compete – with their body, mind and emotions. It is the mind game that can give you:

- ways of thinking that make your physical practice easier and more effective
- ways of thinking that put you in the 'flow state', that 'zone' where everything goes right
- ways of thinking that stop you from being nervous and distracted
- ways of thinking that help you learn more quickly and enjoy your sport more fully

These are the mental skills that we will explore in this book.

Sports psychology is continually evolving and the psychological skills in this book are the result of research and practice over many years. Mentally and physically we continually push the boundaries of what is possible. The Olympics is an international competition dating back 2,000 years. National athletes now perform at levels that would have made them Olympic and world champions 30 years ago. Mental training is now available that formerly was confined to the Olympic élite. These mental skills are not difficult or esoteric – every athlete can use them to improve their performance, expand their skills and increase their enjoyment.

There are five key skills to peak sports performance. The first skill is setting goals. Goals are the rules of the game. Without goals, you do not know why you are playing or how to win. You need to know what you want to achieve and how you want to achieve it. Without a destination you can't begin to move in the right direction – there *is* no right direction. Setting goals gives you direction and focus, both short term and long term.

Just because you want something does not mean you will get it automatically. There is an art to setting goals, a way of making them realistic, motivating and achievable. Part of goal setting is an appraisal of where you are right now. Once you know where you are and where you want to go, you can plan your way from one to the other. This book is a map to guide you.

The second skill is mental rehearsal using all the senses. Mental rehearsal is a consistent pattern of the top performers in every field – sports, the arts, education, even politics. Anything we do in the outside world must first happen in the inside world of our mind. Visualization is usually the most effective way to rehearse mentally, but sight is not your only sense, so visualization is not the only way to practise mentally. You have your own individual way of thinking, so you want to build a mental rehearsal programme that is uniquely yours. You can tailor it to your own goals and way of thinking.

The third skill is the ability to concentrate, to focus and pay attention in the present moment. Athletes use many different words for this: 'concentration', 'flow', 'being in the zone'. When you are there everything goes right, there is no sense of effort or force, everything happens naturally by itself and all you have to do is enjoy it and stop yourself from interfering. We have all had experiences like this and not only in sport. Afterwards we may try to recapture that state and the resulting performance, but come up against a paradox: the harder we try to recapture the state, the further it recedes. Like a Zen riddle, the more you try to grasp it, the more it recedes and you end up grasping at thin air. The only way into the zone is to stop trying and clear away the distractions that are stopping you getting there. One of those distractions is the trying to get there.

The fourth skill is the ability to deal with distractions and anxiety. Distractions come in many forms: the worries we bring to the game, poor environment, bad luck, incompetent umpires, referees and line judges. Not all of these are within our direct control. Some *should* be within our control, but prove tantalizingly elusive, like the internal voices that whisper in our ear and distract us at critical moments. We have to deal with these distractions and manage our energy to play at our best. Too much effort and we become over-anxious and tight. Too much relaxation and we become languid and sloppy. The right balance is not easy to achieve.

The fifth and last skill is to learn from our performance, triumph or disaster. We have to deal with success and failure. Success we want to duplicate and failure we want to avoid. The best athletes make mistakes, but they rarely make the same mistake twice. Dealing with injury is part of this learning. Sport is physical – bodies hit each other at high speed and people do get hurt. No one gets hurt sitting in an armchair thinking (though perhaps if chess is ever classified as a sport and 'chess rage' gets established, even that may no longer be true)!

My work with athletes, mainly golfers and tennis players, has focused on these skills. Most of the time, I have not been telling the athletes what to do as much as clearing away obstacles that stop them being their best. Athletes are usually very aware of what is wrong with their game, but do not pay enough attention to what is right. It is the old story – we take what we can do well for granted and concentrate on what we cannot achieve. Though I have used these five skills in helping athletes, this book is not primarily about coaching others or how to coach. It is primarily about coaching yourself, motivating yourself and knowing what is important to you about your sport.

Skills are useless, however, if you do not put them into action. Theoretical knowledge alone never helped anyone to improve at their sport. Brains learn fast. Bodies are slower. So you need to practise – to repeat an action with the right kind of attention. Practice can make perfect or perfunctory – depending on how you practise. This book will give you exercises for developing the five skills and ideas on how to put them into practice.

Mental skills make you a winner. In a contest between two equally talented individuals or teams, the mentally tougher one will win. Even when one is physically fitter or more skilful, mental skills can turn the game around. Winning is important – although it depends on how you define winning. This is not a book that will tell you how to win at any price. Some prices are too high. I often read of athletes who have ruined their health in pursuit of fitness and the glory of winning. Health and fitness are not the same. Health is how well your body works as a whole – the word 'health' shares the same root as the word 'whole'. Fitness is the ability of the body to work, but once you can work, you can also overwork. Your health is more important than winning any contest. You live with your body 24 hours a day, every day, every year, while a trophy just gathers dust on the mantelpiece. Know your body, befriend it and listen to it. Then it will perform wonders for you.

How to Use this Book

The sequence of mental skills is important, so to get the most from this book, read it in order rather than dipping in and out. It is designed so that the skills build on each other. You cannot make a mental game plan unless you know what you want, so outcomes are first. Next comes mental rehearsal through imagery, followed by concentration – that most elusive and important quality. Balancing effort and energy comes after that and finally there are the skills of learning from your performance and dealing with injury. There are exercises in every section. You can use these to build your own unique mental game plan and focus on the areas of your game that need work. The exercises are indexed *(see page 198)* so you can easily locate which exercise to use in which situation.

You can use this book for any sport, whether it is an individual sport or team sport. When you are a member of a team you have an extra dimension to consider – how to work together with your team-mates so the team as a whole is better than the sum of the parts. All teams have some outstanding individuals, but the most successful teams have a special synergy and a co-ordination. Every team player still does their best, but not just for themselves. This book will also help you to fit into team strategy and ways of thinking.

You may be thinking these skills are not exclusive to sport and you are right. They apply in everyday life, too. As you use these skills to succeed in sport, I hope you will also find wider applications in the rest of your life.

NLP

This book applies some of the insights of neuro-linguistic programming. NLP is the branch of psychology that is particularly well suited to sports performance. It is made up of three words that explain what it does:

neuro	how we think: our neurology
linguistic	words and how we say them: our language
programming	how we act to achieve our results: our goals

NLP helps us understand how great athletes get their results, so you can learn from them to improve in your own way. You do not have to reinvent the wheel. You can use NLP to 'model' your sporting idols or your best performance, to capture those times when you played well and when everything went right, analyse what was happening and use those insights in the future.

NLP also studies how we think; how we create the world we live in, with all its successes and failures, joys and sorrows. Everyone thinks in a unique way. Therefore NLP can help you personalize your mental training and mental rehearsal in a way that other branches of psychology cannot. Too many books on mental training assume that because a particular form of imagery works for some people (or the author), it will work for everybody. It won't, and that may explain some of the common disappointments of mental training. NLP will allow you to design imagery that suits you.

NLP links mind and body. How you think influences how you run, how you breathe, how you feel – and how you feel influences how committed you are, how much energy you have and how motivated you are. Mind and body are two separate words for one experience. Once we know how they influence each other, we can get the greatest result with the least effort.

You need know nothing of NLP in order to benefit from this book. NLP is a means to an end – sporting excellence. But whatever skills you have, NLP can help you make more of them.

There are four principles of NLP:

1 First, *take care of your relationships*. Good relationships with others are obvious, especially with coaches, teammates and colleagues, but also remember the relationships you have within yourself, for example, how you treat your body and how you balance the conflicting demands of your sport, your team and the rest of your life.

2 The second principle is to *know what you want* – to set your goals carefully, to make them as motivating and realistic as possible. All your actions have a purpose, but sometimes what you achieve is not what you set out to achieve.

3 The third principle of NLP is to *pay attention to your senses* – to be sensitive to what you see, hear and feel. They tell you when you are on track to achieve your goals. Part of sports training is to be particularly sensitive to feelings of balance and touch. The best athletes have the greatest physical awareness.

4 Finally, given that you have a goal and you are paying attention to what is happening, the fourth principle is *physical and mental flexibility* – trying different methods to get what you want. There are many athletes and teams that play in a fixed way. They play to their strengths and this may work much of the time, but what happens when your opponent surprises you? Do you have the flexibility to change your plan, to change your game, to do something different in reply? Many athletes do not. Under pressure they do what they do best – only more so. They do it harder, more often and more strongly. Then they lose. Any strength can turn into a weakness if your opponent uses it against you, as the martial arts demonstrate so well. The way to throw an opponent in judo is not to apply brute force to topple them over but to use their own movement against them, to exaggerate it so that the person seems to throw themselves. You just help them on their way.

These NLP principles – good relationships, goal setting, sensitivity, awareness and flexibility – are the same principles that lead to sporting success.

Finally, what about natural talent? Surely some people have more natural ability than others do? Yes. But that does not stop you developing the talent you have. No baby jumps from the cradle, the complete athlete – we all have to learn.

A 'talent' was originally a unit of money. Some people are born into rich families; others make money for themselves. You can earn money, invest what you have, save or even gamble. Likewise, everyone has some talent and you do not know the limit of yours until you develop it. To say someone is naturally talented is a shorthand way of saying that they are very good and you don't know why. Talent does not explain; it describes. Discover how much talent you have and enjoy the search. What counts are your results and the skills that you develop by practice.

This book is for all athletes, amateur and professional who wish to improve their skills and enjoy their sport more. We start together. Where you set the finishing line is up to you.

This book is not designed to substitute for professional fitness or medical advice. It will help you use your mind in the service of your body to enjoy and succeed at your sport. You should seek appropriate medical advice before starting any fitness programme.

Ready... Get Set...

I like the story of the two friends who met to play golf one afternoon. They were both keen golfers and belonged to the same club, but they had never played each other before. The first golfer took his stance and was getting ready to tee off when his friend noticed that the ball he was using looked rather peculiar and, what was more, it was the only one he had.

'Just a minute,' he said, 'before we start, don't you need another golf ball?'

'Nope, this one will be enough,' replied the first golfer with a smirk.

'Are you sure?' asked his friend. 'What happens if you lose it?'

'Aha, this is a very special golf ball. I won't lose it, so I don't need another one.'

'I'm not putting your game down, but it's easy to lose a ball. We all do it. What happens if the ball goes in that lake?'

'That's OK, this special golf ball floats, so I'll be able to get it back.'

'Suppose you hit it into the trees and it gets lost in the bushes?'

'No problem. This ball has a homing beacon. I can locate it within 1,000 yards.'

'Hmm. OK,' said his friend with an edge beginning to creep into his voice, 'let's say our game lasts into the evening and you land in the sand trap on the eighteenth. What then?'

'Aha! This ball glows in the dark. I can always find it, however dark it gets.'

'That is one amazing ball,' said his friend. 'I guess it really is all you need. Where on Earth did you get it anyway?'

'Oh, I found it.'

We are all looking for the magic ingredient for success: a mental game plan, a special technique or practice regime guaranteed to lift our game and help us win. However, if there were such an answer, then everyone would use it. And something that helps everyone equally helps no one.

You have to find your own answer and it must come from your own efforts by making the most of the mental and physical skills you have.

The Three Factors of Sports Success

Sporting success has three parts:

1 *Fitness* – Fitness is the ability of the body to perform work. Mental skills will not help you if your body doesn't obey you. Fitness puts you in the game stronger, faster, longer. You may be a tough, talented tennis player for example, with immense powers of concentration, but if you cannot last more than a three-stroke rally, a fitter opponent will probably beat you, although you may be the better player in every other aspect of the game.
2 *Technical skills* – These are your sports skills, for example putting accurately in golf, serving well in tennis or controlling a spinning football. You build these specific skills by consistent practice.
3 *Mental skills* – Mental skills help you gain the physical skills you need. They direct your energy and motivate you towards your goals. They help you build precise mental rehearsal techniques that make your physical practice more effective. They help you focus your attention and give you the will to win. They help you balance your energy and build the mental toughness you need to withstand the pressures of competition. They give you confidence and the belief in yourself that makes you a winner.

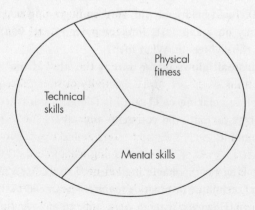

Figure 1.1: Natural sports ability

You need all three skills in different proportions depending on the sport. For example, marathon running depends far more on physical fitness than bowling does. Tennis and golf need a greater variety of technical skills than field events. All sports, however, demand some degree of skill and physical fitness. This is the price of admission you pay in order to play. But the mental skills give you the edge; they make the difference when fitness and physical skill are level. Everything else being equal, the player who is the more mentally skilled will be the winner.

Take a moment to think about your own sport. How do these three components fit in? How much does your sport depend on physical fitness? How much technical skill is involved? How can the mental skills make a difference?

Fitness

Fitness is the ability of the body to perform work. Everybody is fit to some extent – it comes with having a physical body – but how fit you are is another question. At one extreme the couch potato pants while climbing one flight of stairs before collapsing in the armchair with the next packet of crisps or Danish pastry. At the other extreme, the long-distance runner covers several miles before tucking into morning muesli.

To get fit you need to exercise. As you gradually increase your level of activity with longer, more frequent and more intense exercise, so you increase your body's ability to work and hence your fitness. This is true whatever level of fitness you have to begin with. Many people are put off exercising because the word conjures up images of blood, sweat and tears on a running machine, under a large banner reading, 'No pain, no gain.'

What sort of reaction do you have to the word 'exercise'?

Do you think of it as a pleasant activity or something you have to do?

If you don't like the word 'exercise', what about the word 'activity'? Exercise *is* activity, using your body over and above its normal resting level. Never let a mere word stop you doing what you want to do.

Exercise is not only something you need to do to get fit, it is also essential for good health. Inactivity is dangerous. Moderate frequent exercise counters the most widespread effects of ageing, including excess body fat, high blood pressure, poor blood sugar balance and higher levels of fat and cholesterol in the blood. It decreases your risk of stroke, coronary heart disease and colon cancer. You can get these benefits from 30 minutes or more of moderate activity at least five days a week or at least 20 minutes of vigorous activity three or more days a week (though you need more than this to be fit).

Exercise is not only good for you, it is also enjoyable. When you exercise you trigger the release of chemicals called endorphins into the bloodstream. Endorphins are released at nerve endings and they affect mood, perception of pain, memory and learning. They are the body's 'happy chemicals' – natural pain relievers which have a similar chemical structure to morphine. They work as analgesics and they make you feel good too – much better than aspirin! They are released during orgasm and when you laugh. If endorphins were synthetic drugs, they would probably be illegal or tightly controlled by central government and only available on prescription. Yet you can have them for nothing more than 20 minutes of exercise!

The more you exercise, the fitter you become – but only up to a point. Beware of over-exercising in the pursuit of fitness. It is possible to have too much of a good thing. You should always allow at least one day a week to rest and recover from the effects of exercise and it is a good idea to have a day off after any particularly vigorous day. You need the recovery time to get the benefit of the exercise. Without adequate recovery time you will lose the effects of exercise, weaken your immune system and become tired, listless and prone to illness. Other effects of overtraining are loss of appetite, difficulty sleeping, persistent muscle soreness and feeling stale. Fitness is only one part of health. You can be healthy but not very fit, or fit and not very healthy.

Whatever your present fitness level, you can build an exercise plan to increase it. The less fit you are to begin with, the greater your potential to become fit. You may be satisfied with your present level of fitness, but better opponents will demand you are fitter as well as more skilful.

Fitness has four components – speed, stamina, strength and suppleness; the 'Four S' formula. Different sports need a different balance of these, just as a good cocktail needs different amounts of the right ingredients. *(See Appendix I for ways to develop your fitness and exercise programme.)*

Get fit to play sport – don't play sport to get fit!

Technical Skill

Every sport also needs a certain amount of technical skill – the ability to make complex movements fluently, consistently and correctly. Sports coaching concentrates on this aspect. You improve by practising the physical movements you need in your sport so that they become easy and habitual. As you practise the physical movements, you also practise the thinking that goes with them.

Many people have an idea that practice means a kind of rote repetition in a non-competitive situation, so it does not matter. Somehow it seems practice is not 'real'. My dictionary defines practice as 'repetition or exercise of an activity in order to gain skill...' Practice is an abstract noun, you have to flesh it out to make sense of it:

What are you practising?
How are you practising?
What are you paying attention to when you practise?

Practice by itself means nothing. Practice makes perfect, perfunctory, poor or painful, depending on how you practise. When you practise your sport you are doing two things:

■ First you are building reliable mental representations about how to move your body. The idea forms and guides your actions. That is why you can use mental training to practise more effectively, as we shall see.
■ Secondly, you are consolidating the muscle memory, repeating the same movement until it becomes a habit.

What you repeat has to be correct. If you repeat a poor movement then you get very fluent at that poor movement. Wrong practice limits your ability and sets you back even more because it is harder to undo a habit than to build one. Not only will you have to practise the more effective movement, but also you will have to dismantle the old habit and that takes more time.

So, the first rule of practice is not to practise a movement unless you are sure it is the right one. How will you know? You have to get a picture of what the correct movement looks like, a sense of what it feels like and then make your movement to reproduce that sight and feeling.

The easiest way to build that initial correct idea is to get some good coaching. Once you know what to do, then you can practise it. It is worth making a small investment of time and money at the beginning to start on the right track. If you do not have a good coach, then you need a good model, someone you can copy, someone you can learn from.

Don't practise until you get it right – practise until you can't get it wrong.

Figure 1.2: Learning a technical skill

Learning a skill traditionally has four steps. You can probably trace your learning path through these for your sport:

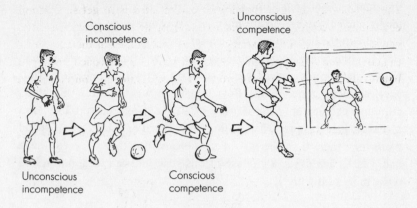

Figure 1.3: The four stages of traditional learning

1 You start from *unconscious incompetence* – you don't know and you don't know you don't know. To begin with you don't know anything about your sport. Then something kindles your interest, maybe you see it on television, or play it at school, or your family and friends play. Perhaps someone you admire plays and you want to be like that person. Maybe you fall into it by accident and enjoy it.

2 Then you come to the second stage – *conscious incompetence*. You start to play, but you are not very good. There is a lot to learn. However, you learn quickly, you get immediate results and you are motivated.

3 Next you enter the stage of *conscious competence*. You have skill, but you need to concentrate. This is a satisfying stage of learning, but the better you are, the more effort is needed to make a noticeable gain, so it is more difficult to improve.

4 Finally you come to *unconscious competence*. At this stage your skill is habitual. You do not have to think about it; you play most of your game without having to decide consciously what to do and how to do it. This is the goal of practice. The more skills you have in unconscious competence, the more mind space you have to learn other skills.

Different parts of your game may be in different stages. For example, a tennis player may serve with unconscious competence, but their backhand down the line may only be consciously competent.

Beyond these four stages lies *mastery*. Mastery is more than unconscious competence; it has an extra aesthetic dimension. Your playing looks good, it has flow. I believe we all enter this state, although perhaps only for seconds at a time. Great players like John McEnroe, Pete Sampras, Nick Faldo, David Owen or Allan Donald spend more time there than the rest of us mortals. However once you have had a taste, a whisper, a glimpse of this state you can recapture it and make more of it with NLP.

This traditional way of learning is not the only way. We do not learn everything so consciously and systematically. You did not learn to talk like this, nor all the complicated social rules, rituals and ways of behaving. You learned these by watching other people and copying them, often not understanding what you were copying. This is a more intuitive way of learning and the basis of modelling. It is also very effective. When we are young, we model indiscriminately. We see adults and in our childlike eyes, they are like gods, so we copy them. As we grow up we realize that these adults have their quirks, foibles and limitations and we are more careful about who we model. Modelling is one way of accelerated learning because it accelerates through the two middle stages (conscious incompetence and conscious competence) and goes more quickly to unconscious competence at the cost of conscious understanding.

Accelerated learning in sport can happen when we copy great athletes without understanding exactly what they are doing. This happens quite naturally. Think back to a time when you were watching your sport, either live or on television, and you were paying full attention, following the game, mind and body. People may have been talking nearby, but you paid no attention to them. You flinched and moved, twisted and turned in response to what happened. If you were watching a golfer addressing a difficult putt to win a match, you were likely to be quiet, attentive, judging the distance with him. You may even have 'mirrored' the athlete with your own small muscle movements. Watching a sport teaches you a lot about it. You have only to see two children in a game, one who has watched it before and the other has not, to see the difference it makes.

Watch carefully the athletes you admire. If you have a coach, watch what they do as well as following their instructions, then you can learn from them at two levels. The first level is what they say. The second, a deeper and more influential level, is what they do. Their movements help you build those mental pictures and feelings you need for your sports technique. The more good role models you watch, the more you will learn at this accelerated level. Watching the sport on television can help you improve!

Later we will be using mental imagery to make this modelling process even more powerful.

The Mind Game

Mental skills support your physical skills, for technique is both mental and physical. You can't hit a ball with your mind, but you can't hit the ball without your mind either.

Talent = fitness + physical skills x mental skills
T = F + (P x CEW)

Mental skills have three parts:

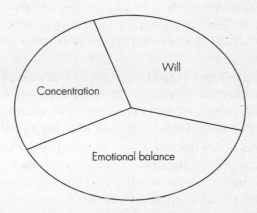

Figure 1.4: Mental skills

1   *Concentration* – This is the ability to be in the moment, to direct
    your attention to what is important without being diverted. It is the
    royal road to the flow state. When you concentrate, you cut out all
    distractions, whether they come from the outside (for example,
    officials or crowd noise) or the inside (for example, internal voices
    saying how hard or easy it is to win).

2   *Emotional balance* – This is your energy balance, how well you
    walk the tightrope between too much effort and too much
    relaxation, both physical and mental. It determines how effective
    and efficient you are in your sport. Too much effort wastes energy,
    tires you out and makes it difficult to concentrate. Too little effort
    and you lose power; your playing is weak. The pivot is your
    physical balance and emotional state.

3   *Will* – This is your strength of purpose, how easily and strongly
    you can channel your mental and physical energy. Will is your
    determination to win; it acts as a focus for your emotional energy.
    At its best, it is like a laser that can cut through steel and at its
    weakest like a torch with a faulty battery unable to penetrate the
    shadows. It is the difference between involvement and commitment.
    You are involved just by being there. You are committed when you
    would not be anywhere else. It is like the old joke about making a
    breakfast of bacon and eggs. In this meal, the chicken is involved
    and the pig is committed.

Martina Navratilova spent many years playing tennis well, but not
sufficiently well to break through to stardom. Looking back at this time
she commented, 'I didn't really train hard. Then I finally realized
I couldn't just rely on what everyone called my natural abilities. I
learned to work and conscientiously to truly play at my capabilities.'
She was able to multiply her talent by increasing her mental skills.

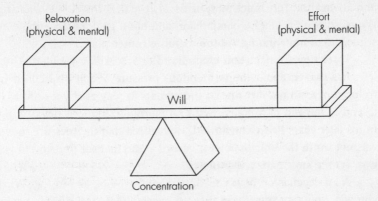

Figure 1.5: Emotional balance

Winning and Losing

What gives the greatest motivation and commitment? What is one of the greatest reasons for playing? Winning. Winning is a great feeling, which is especially satisfying if you have worked hard for it and played well. Everyone loves a winner. We may sympathize with and admire the 'good loser', but losing is disappointing. The trophy has only room for one name at a time.

Winning is important and it's right to set goals to win. However there is a dark side too, because when you only think in terms of winning and losing, then it has to be one or the other. You risk creating a black and white world where you are either top or nowhere. There can be only one winner, but many losers. The danger is to think that you are a loser if you do not beat everyone else.

The great basketball coach John Wooden avoided using the words 'win' or 'lose' during the basketball season. He used to say that he never mentioned those words because they took the players' attention off their work. He would refuse to say that his team beat the other team, he used to say that they 'outscored' them.

The *idea* of winning can be a distraction from playing your best and *actually* winning. Winning is important but not all-important. The will to win is different from wanting to win at all costs. Putting too much importance on winning at all costs can indeed exact a cost – drug abuse, persistent injury, illness, early retirement, disillusionment

and ill health. Too much emphasis also makes losing devastating.
Winning then becomes a compulsion and not a goal, because the consequences of not winning are too awful to contemplate.

Three times Wimbledon champion Boris Becker, a wonderful athlete, has spoken about the tremendous pressure he put on himself by
trying to remain number one in the world: 'To play as if your life were
to end at the end of a match, with no morning after ... is devastating.'
In his later years Becker mellowed. He realized that the pressure to win
was not worth the unhappiness it caused – and that the pressure to win
was, for the most part, self-inflicted.

A lot depends on how you think about winning and losing. When
you win, you gain something through merit. What you gain may come
from the outside – applause, respect, a prize, a cup or a certificate.
From the inside, you always gain a good feeling. You also gain important intangibles like pride, self-respect and increased confidence. All
these are worth having. Losing, on the other hand, seems to imply you
have lost something, in other words you had something and now you
don't. However, that is not true in sport unless you are defending a
title, which you might lose to another competitor. If you are not
defending a title:

You never had anything in the first place, so you can't lose it.

When you have nothing to lose, you are free to win.

Winning and losing are not opposites. It may seem that if you are
not a winner, then you must be a loser. But such polar thinking is mis-
leading and distracting. Polar thinking gives you a world that consists
only of a North and South Pole without a temperate zone between
them.

There can only be winners in sport – you can't lose, you can only fail to
win on a particular occasion at a particular time.

If winning is narrowly defined as coming first, in front of all the other
competitors, it becomes overridingly important. Then you are in a bind,
because second place is the same as last place. You have to avoid
losing, *not* coming first becomes too important. 'I mustn't lose' does not
have the same effect as 'I must win.' Say them to yourself and notice
the difference. When you say 'I must win', you think of winning. When

you say 'I mustn't lose', you think of losing, not winning. That disturbs your concentration and puts you under pressure. You don't want to lose, but the thought won't go away. It can make you snatch defeat from the jaws of victory.

The mind game is particularly important in golf. Here, everything is concentrated into a split second of action. Even the slightest miscue can make the difference between a fine shot and a sandy graveyard. The American Greg Norman is an excellent golfer with immense skill, but he developed a reputation in the late 1980s for not being able to take pressure. He would be with the tournament leaders but then fade in the last round. He had a really strong desire to win that made him susceptible to the pressure of polar thinking and this came through in a dramatic way in the 1996 Masters Tournament held in Augusta. Norman played wonderfully for the first three days, shooting a course record on the first day, and at the beginning of the final day he was six strokes ahead of his nearest rival, Nick Faldo. On that Sunday morning, as he strode out to finish, people were saying that there was no way that he could lose, the very idea was ridiculous. And yet, perhaps this added to the pressure on him. On that Sunday he was a different golfer. He played badly. His pre shot routine became drawn out and his technique looked uncertain. Nick Faldo played steady, strong and excellent golf. He overtook Norman and won by five strokes. On the day he beat Norman by 11 strokes, a huge margin for one day's play between two top golfers. What made the difference? I suggest it was that Faldo had nothing to lose and everything to win. Norman had nothing to win and everything to lose. Faldo had winning in mind and Norman had losing in mind.

Exercise 1: Winning and Losing

Here is an exercise to explore how you think of winning and losing in your sport.

First imagine yourself as 'losing', being beaten by your opponent or the opposing team.

What sort of scene comes into your mind?
If you have a mental picture, what sort of picture is it?
How bright is it?

How colourful?
Is it a moving picture or a still picture?
How fast is the movement?
How big is the picture?
How far away is it from your field of vision?
Are there any sounds?
If so, how loud are they?
Are you talking to yourself about losing?
If so, what are you saying and in what tone of voice?
How do you feel about losing?

Write down your answers.

Now imagine yourself winning, coming first, beating your opponent or the other team. Go through the same questions and write down the answers.

There is an example below of a complete answer.

Picture	Sounds	Feelings
Winning	*Winning*	*Winning*
Big bright picture, directly in front of me, coloured, moving. I see myself holding up a trophy and people cheering.	People cheering and applauding. I hear myself saying, 'Well done!' quite loudly and clearly.	Feel good, proud of myself, a warm feeling in my stomach, a light feeling in my head.
Losing	*Losing*	*Losing*
A picture of myself looking dejected – a smaller picture, darker. The picture is still in front of me, but closer.	No sound except my voice saying something like, 'Huh!'	Tension in my jaw and eyes. An empty feeling in my stomach.

Now you have a fuller idea of what winning and losing mean to you.

What are the differences?

What happens if you think of 'not winning' instead of losing? Do you get the same pictures, sounds and feelings as you did for 'losing'?

Is there any middle ground between winning and losing in your mental pictures, sounds and feelings?

Remember *you* create the ideas from the words' and then you create the feelings in response to those ideas. When you think of winning and losing differently, you can create different pictures, sounds and feelings and then you will have different feelings in response. *You* create your feelings, not the words.

Making a narrow definition of winning and then striving for it at all costs is dangerous and counterproductive. A winner who *has* to be a winner will always feel insecure and vulnerable. One of the reasons for this is that you can't *try* to make yourself win. Playing your best is the way to win and you cannot force yourself to play well. The more you try to force yourself, the more pressure you feel and the worse you will play. When you are in the middle of a game, winning and losing are in the future and thinking of them distracts you from giving your best in the present moment, which is when the game will be won or lost. The pressure is self-defeating, like pulling yourself up by your own boot-laces. So your opponent does not defeat you – you defeat yourself. But when you are unattached to winning and losing, you free yourself to play at your best.

If you are afraid of losing, then you dare not win either.

Bjorn Borg (five times Wimbledon tennis champion)

Here is another exercise to clarify what winning means to you.

Exercise 2: The Meaning of Winning

What is it like to win?

Think back to a time when you won a match. What did that get for you?

If there was a trophy, what did it represent?

What is your definition of winning?

Make a list of all the things you get from winning, both external (for example, prizes, congratulations) and internal (for example, confidence and self-esteem).

Do you have to beat everyone else to get those things?

Winning means overcoming an obstacle, so there are two ways of thinking about winning:

■ The first is overcoming an outside obstacle – the other competitors. This is winning defined from the outside.

■ Then there is winning defined on the inside, when you overcome an obstacle that you have decided on. It could be your opponent, it could be a personal limitation, it could be breaking a personal record, regardless of the result of the game. Your goals determine whether you win on the inside.

You may not always win on the outside, but you can make sure that you always win something on the inside by attaining some goal, or some personal best. That way, you win whenever you get what you set out to achieve.

Polar thinking defines winning externally and makes winning and losing mutually exclusive. Having just two possibilities like that can be confusing. It makes me think of the time I drove in Mexico. Mexican traffic lights change from red to green suddenly without warning. Immediately there is a roar as the traffic accelerates away. Most of the drivers have been slipping the clutch waiting for the moment. Some cars stall. Woe betide any pedestrian caught trying to cross the road! This is bad enough, but imagine what it would be like without an amber light between green and red – no room for error. What should you do when approaching a green light? Slow down? Speed up? Just dither? You would either have to play it very safe or risk having an accident. Road safety demands an amber light.

Having a 'win or lose' mentality is just like having only a mental red and green light. You need the amber between because it acts as a protection and stops you either having to go very carefully or risk a meltdown like Greg Norman at Atlanta. The amber light is like the 'Get set' at the beginning of a race between the 'Ready!' and the 'Go!' It would be much harder to start racing smoothly if the assembled runners did not know when 'Go!' was coming. There would be a lot of false starts and if the athletes held back to avoid a false start, then they would risk a poor start.

Excuses, Excuses

When losing becomes too important, then excuses start to multiply. Have you ever been in the situation where you start to make excuses for defeat – in advance? You sneeze and think, 'Well, I am not at my best. I have a cold. I'll probably lose.' Anything can be an excuse, because conditions are never ideal. Sometimes I find myself in the bizarre position where I know my excuse before I know the result! But whenever I have relied on excuses, I have always felt that I let myself down.

If you know your excuse beforehand, then you are going to need it.

In other words, you have defeated yourself before you even started. You are expecting to lose. Much better to act as if there are no excuses. Anticipate what could go wrong and deal with it beforehand instead of letting it become an issue. Go out and do your best whatever the conditions, even if your excuse is a really good one. Rather than being ready with an excuse like 'I had a cold so I didn't play my best. What do you expect?', take a big dose of vitamin C and have an early night. Rather than being ready with 'I didn't play my best because my leg is giving me trouble', take precautions in advance. (You might also consider missing the match. Is it worth it?) Rather than using an excuse on the lines of 'I have a lot of worries on my mind', recognize that you have a lot happening in your life at the moment and make extra mental preparations to maintain your concentration in the game. Instead of 'I was caught in a traffic jam and was late so I had to rush with no warm up', set off early so you will not be in a rush. You will find this approach is strangely reassuring. *You* take responsibility; there is no one and nothing to blame.

Of course conditions may be difficult and may affect your game. There may be an excellent excuse to be had. This approach will not dispense with the cold, the traffic jam or the injury, but it will give you control, choice and responsibility. It will also mean that whatever happens, you will not walk away from the game saying 'If only. . .', surely one of the saddest phrases in the English language.

Think of the kind of excuses you use to yourself and others. Do you have any favourites? Do any come up consistently? What could you do to change that situation? Sometimes miraculously, when you decide there are no more excuses whatever happens, the world stops providing you with nasty surprises that could justify them.

Your Two Opponents

Win or lose, you have two opponents in every game. The first one is your real opponent on the outside. They should be a worthy opponent, one who brings out the best in you. There is little satisfaction in losing badly to a player who is very much better than you – nor in easily beating a player who is very much worse than you. Neither game helps you very much. Also, it is not satisfying to win if you feel that your opponent is holding back, not giving their best or deliberately playing weakly. We like to win, but we want a genuine win. It matters how we win. So we rely on our opponent – their skill determines how skilful we can be.

Being on court with an opponent is a strange business. You are totally out for yourself to win a match, yet you're dependent on your opponent to some degree for the type of match it is and how well you play. You need your opponent – without her you do not exist.

Martina Navratilova

Your second opponent is yourself, or more exactly your limitations. This is a cunning and tricky opponent who will try all sorts of tactics on you: limiting beliefs, lack of focus, inertia and distracting self-talk. This opponent knows exactly what will distract you. You may be halfway to defeat before even meeting your outer opponent, because the inner opponent can drain up to 50 per cent of your skill.

To win on the outside, you have to win the inner mind game with your inner opponent. The more soundly you defeat the inner opponent, the more successful you will be against the outer one. When you do not cope with the inner one, the outer one will cause even more of a problem.

Have you ever been 'psyched' out of a game? You were winning, or at least level, and your opponent started doing something that distracted you. Maybe they did it intentionally, maybe not. If your opponent loses their temper and glares at you in contempt, that can be distracting. It usually means they are worried and are looking for an ally – they are trying to recruit your inner opponent to play on their side. Don't let them! Your outer opponent cannot play mind games on you without co-operation from your inner opponent.

Commitment

You need to be tough to beat both your opponents, whatever level you compete at. Mental toughness comes from a strong will that fires you with the desire to succeed, to work at your sport with a sense of purpose, to be able to set your goals and stick with them. It gives you the ability to keep your emotions in check, at least until after the game. It is a very rare athlete (John McEnroe the tennis player is one), who can be angry and then resume his game with a fierce concentration as if nothing had happened. For most people nothing breaks concentration like strong emotion, and once broken, it is hard to regain. Mental toughness also means committing yourself – putting yourself whole-heartedly into your game. You commit to succeed and once you are committed, you are motivated to succeed and that motivation can produce extraordinary results.

Tiger Woods is generally acknowledged to be an outstandingly talented golfer. He won the Masters in Augusta in splendid fashion in 1998, but he had played the course as an amateur twice before and got nowhere. The year he won, he had turned professional and while he has great talent, his commitment to winning led him to make some remarkable preparations. He studied videotapes of past tournaments at Augusta for six months before the tournament began. He watched the tapes, studied the shots and realized that the only way to win at Augusta was to be good on the greens. This was where the winners always had the edge. When he studied the tapes further he realized that nearly every green sloped from front to back. It is much easier to putt up a hill than down a hill – you have more control. So he devised a simple strategy – he would aim to land his ball short of the hole every time. This would give him an easier uphill putt. And he studied the greens so closely that he knew exactly the best place to land the ball for the easiest uphill putt on every green. His strategy worked perfectly. He never took more than two putts on any green and finished 13 points ahead of the field – the biggest margin ever achieved in that tournament. His commitment led to his painstaking preparation, which gave him confidence and belief in himself.

It often seems that winning athletes manage by talent alone, but we do not see all the preparation that has made their performance so good. That preparation comes from commitment, confidence, self-belief and their mental and physical practice. A major part of 'talent' is a capacity for hard work.

'Commitment' and 'motivation' are both abstract nouns – they do not exist, the energy to work is what is real. Luckily, commitment gives you energy. It is the mental equivalent of physical fitness. It is the appetite for and ability to do mental work over long periods – not just what is enjoyable, but what needs to be done. There are probably parts of your sport that you enjoy more than others, and so you spend more time on them. However, success comes from working on all the aspects – like a chain, your game is only as strong as its weakest link. A good opponent will put pressure on every link and once they have found your weak spot, they will keep testing it.

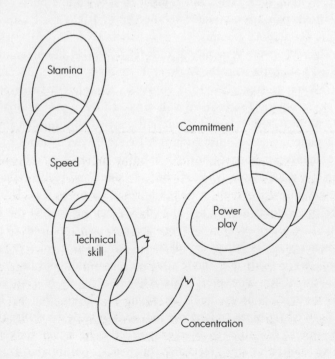

Figure 1.6: Your chain of skills

Think of it like driving a car. You don't think, 'Well, my favourite part of driving is applying the brakes and the accelerator. Changing gear is boring, I think I'll leave that out.' Your driving will be good if all the pieces fit together. You won't get to accelerate or brake unless you use the gears and you might have to apply the brakes hard and fast if you do not look in the mirror!

Exercise 3: Enjoying your Sport

What parts of your sport do you enjoy the most?
What parts are you most motivated to work on?
Why do you enjoy these parts?
What do you get from the parts of the sport that you enjoy?
Are there any parts of your sport that you do not enjoy?

What are the greatest strengths of your game?
What are the greatest weaknesses of your game?
How does what you enjoy doing relate to your strengths and weaknesses?
How could working on the parts that you do not enjoy give you the same benefits?
What is the connection between those parts you do enjoy and those you do not enjoy?

Here's an example. I play squash. I enjoy practising forehand and backhand drives down the wall. I am good at them. I enjoy them because it is satisfying to hit the ball hard, hear the thump as it meets the racket and see it speed on its way to the back of the court. These shots put my opponent under pressure and may win the point. I do not enjoy 'shadowing' – an exercise where I move from the middle of the court first to one side of the court then to the other, pretending to hit the ball. I find it tiring and unsatisfying because I don't hit the ball; I am only practising the movement. But when I thought about it, I realized that shadowing is an essential part of being able to hit powerful strokes. Unless I could get to the ball and position myself, I couldn't time the shot. Very rarely in a game do I have the luxury of a ball that sits up and begs to be hit. I have to chase it. Now I practise shadowing with more pleasure because I have connected it to my enjoyment of playing a good drive.

Your Internal Coach

As well as an internal opponent, we all have an internal coach – the part of us that gets us moving and motivated. The coach's most difficult job is to get us to do those things that we are not so keen on doing.

How does your internal coach motivate you? Some are bullies – they shout at you, telling you that you must do something, you should do it and there will be dire consequences if you don't do it. They show you intimidating mental pictures of what you *have* to do. This is not good psychology.

The strongest commitment and motivation come from your values. When something is important to you, you want to do it. You are drawn to it. It is much more pleasant to be drawn to something than to be pushed into it.

Try this little thought experiment. Imagine someone pushing you from behind towards something. What happens? You probably stiffen and resist, even if what you are pushed towards is pleasant, because you have no control over the push. Now imagine being drawn towards that same thing – much smoother and more pleasant.

So, let yourself be drawn to what you want, not pushed into it. All coaches, internal and external, who appeal to the players' values usually get better results, for the players are more motivated. Authoritarian coaches make it harder for the players to be motivated.

If your internal coach is a bit of a bully, use the next exercise to educate it.

Exercise 4: Educating your Internal Coach

Think about how you motivate yourself to practise. Take some part of your practice that normally you don't like doing.

Do you hear an internal voice?
What is it saying?
How does it talk to you?

Does it talk to you as if you were another person by saying, '*You* do this,' or does it say, '*I* do this'?

Try both ways. Which one is more motivating?

Next, notice if your internal coach uses words like 'must', 'should' or 'ought to'. If it does, then change them to 'can' or 'will'.

So, for example, 'I must practise my tackling' becomes 'I can practise my tackling' or 'I will practise my tackling.'

Say the new versions to yourself and notice if it makes a difference to how you feel.

Do you have mental pictures? If you do, notice whether they show you *doing* the task, or *having done* the task.

It is usually more motivating to think about the task done than the doing of it. Think about the benefits you will get when it is done, not the effort of doing it.

Some internal coaches will show you or tell you about the dire consequences of not doing the task, for example, 'If you don't practise your tackling you'll be useless and you'll be dropped from the team.' Educate your internal coach to show you the positive benefits, for example, 'When I practise my tackling, I'll be better at it and have a much better chance of being picked for the team.'

Don't let your internal coach demotivate you by showing you the enormity of the task. Take it in easy stages. For example, if you are beginning a two-hour practice session, remember that you will be doing only one hour before you get a break. Don't think of the whole session as one activity. Any task will look overwhelming if you think about doing it all at once and even the largest task will be manageable if you break it into small enough pieces.

To sum up, motivate yourself by:

- saying 'I can...' or 'I will...' and not 'I must...' or 'I should...'
- picturing the task done, not you doing it
- thinking of the benefits of doing it rather than the unpleasant consequences of not doing it
- breaking the task down into manageable chunks

The final exercise in this chapter is to remind you of what is important about your sport. When you have played a sport for some time, you can forget what drew you to it and the enjoyment you get from it.

Exercise 5: Why You Play

Think back to when you started playing your sport.

> What was it that attracted you to it?
> How often do you play?
> Would you play more often if you could?
> What do you get from it now that is important to you?
> What have you learned and whom have you met through playing?

Make a list of the physical, mental, emotional and social benefits that you get from your sport. Your list is a unique group of benefits – your reasons for playing.

What would it be like if you remembered these benefits whenever you played? Perhaps there is a word or a sentence or an image that sums them up for you. Maybe you have a trophy or a photograph. Use that to remind yourself of why you play.

A key to motivation and improvement is setting challenging and worthwhile goals. Your goals are the targets you aim to hit; they define the rules of the inner game against your internal opponent and set the scene for imagery, concentration and the right balance of energy. The next step in your mental game plan is how to set your goals. This is the focus of the next chapter.

CHAPTER ONE SUMMARY

The three factors of sports success are:

1   *Fitness:* the ability of your body to perform work
There are four types of fitness:

Speed: the time it takes to complete a movement
Stamina: the ability to maintain speed and/or strength over time
Strength: the maximum force you can exert in a muscle
contraction
Suppleness: the ability to stretch muscle groups

Exercise has great health benefits, but to build fitness you need
aerobic exercise of sufficient intensity, frequency and duration.

2   *Technical skill:* the specific skills that relate to your sport
Traditionally we learn these in four stages:

Unconscious incompetence: We don't know what we don't know.
Conscious incompetence: We know that we are not very good.
Conscious competence: We improve the skill, but it still needs
attention.
Unconscious competence: The skill is consistent and habitual.

Modelling and accelerated learning can take you to a fifth stage:
mastery.

3   *Mental skills*
Focus: the ability to concentrate in the moment
Emotional balance: the balance between relaxation and effort,
both physical and mental
Will: your mental energy, your determination to win or to achieve
your goal because it is important to you

Will depends on energy, motivation, commitment and confidence in your ability to win. You must want to win, but not so much that it interferes with your game. When winning and losing become too important it is difficult to play well. Paying too much attention to losing can destroy the concentration you need to win.

Take responsibility for whatever happens. Do not prepare or use excuses even if they are justified.

You have two opponents: your real opponent and your own limitations.

Commitment is the mental equivalent of fitness – the ability to work. It gives you energy and motivation.
    Commitment has three aspects:

1 Intensity – how intensely you work (mental strength)
2 Duration – how long you work (mental stamina)
3 Activity – what you do

The greatest motivation comes from enjoying and succeeding in your sport.
    A good coach (internal or external) will:

■ use the language of possibilities ('you can'), rather than language of necessity ('you should')
■ have a pleasant tonality
■ motivate by achievement, not by avoiding unpleasant consequences
■ represent the benefits of the task done, not the doing of it
■ break the task into manageable pieces

Goals and How to Get Them

What do you want to achieve in your sport? This will be your goal. Have you ever systematically thought about your goals?

Every game has its own goal and that determines the rules of the game. You also need personal goals for your mental game plan, otherwise it is like playing football without any goalposts – you will be aimlessly kicking around. Goals co-ordinate and direct your movements during the game, between games and in the long term. Goals direct your attention; they harness your energy and spur you on to better performances and winning strategies. They give you a standard by which to measure your progress. They motivate you, challenge you and give you a purpose as well as a sense of achievement and pride.

Goal setting makes sense intuitively and there are many sports psychology studies that show how effective it is. One study of lacrosse players during a complete season found that players who set goals improved according to nearly all performance measures when compared to a control group. A survey of leading sports psychology consultants working with the United States Olympic Athletes reported goal setting was the technique most often used to help the athletes. Goal setting works for every level of sports achievement, not just for élite athletes. It is the essential first step to improved performance – provided of course that you act on your goals.

How you set goals is as important as the goals you set. Positive thinking alone (while better than negative thinking) is no use without goals to give it substance. Goals are often called 'dreams with deadlines'.

So, first set your goals. Then decide the strategy – how you are going to achieve them. This chapter will help you to set motivating, realistic and achievable goals

---

The Benefits of Goal Setting

Goals offer:

enjoyment
a way of measuring progress
challenge
motivation
focus
a sense of purpose

Your Key Performance Qualities

A goal is what you want to achieve; you don't have it right now. When you set a goal you create a gap between where you are and where you want to be, and you commit yourself to that journey. The joy of sport is in the journey as well as the achievement of arriving at the goal.

Before you can set goals, you need to find out exactly where you are now. Here is a short questionnaire for you to discover your strengths and potentials in your sport and in the mind game that goes with it.

Exercise 6: Mental Skills Questionnaire

Mark your response for each question.

Mark 5 if you strongly agree with the statement.
Mark 4 if you agree most of the time.
Mark 3 if you are not sure or you think the statement is true about half the time.
Mark 2 if you are uncertain or you think the statement is true less than half the time.
Mark 1 if you disagree.

Imagery

	Agree	Unsure		Disagree	
I work with imagery already.	5	4	3	2	1
I find it easy to make vivid mental images.	5	4	3	2	1
I can easily create and remember feelings mentally.	5	4	3	2	1
I can hear sounds in my mind easily.	5	4	3	2	1
I can easily control my mental images.	5	4	3	2	1

Now write some short answers to these questions:

What aspects of mental imagery are you good at?
What aspects of mental imagery do you feel would benefit from more
    work?

Concentration

	Agree	Unsure		Disagree	
I already work on my powers of concentration.	5	4	3	2	1
I find it easy to keep my concentration in a game.	5	4	3	2	1
I am rarely distracted by my opponent.	5	4	3	2	1

| I am rarely distracted by my own thoughts. | 5 | 4 | 3 | 2 | 1 |

| I can keep the same quality of concentration throughout a game, whatever happens. | 5 | 4 | 3 | 2 | 1 |

Note down the answers to these questions:

Where are you good at keeping your concentration?
Where are you not so good?

Emotional Balance

	Agree		Unsure		Disagree
I find it easy to relax after my sport.	5	4	3	2	1
I rarely feel anxious in a game.	5	4	3	2	1
I rarely get injured.	5	4	3	2	1
I can easily summon energy and commitment for a game.	5	4	3	2	1
I do not feel unduly anxious and uncomfortable before a game.	5	4	3	2	1

Some other questions:

What helps you control your energy before a game?
What helps you control your energy during a game?
Where could you make your energy balance better to improve your game?

Give yourself a score out of 25 for each aspect and convert that into a percentage by multiplying by 4.

For example, when I did this questionnaire I scored 21 for imagery, which means 84 per cent. I scored 14 for concentration, which is 56 per cent, and 17 for relaxation/tension, that is 68 per cent. So, the area that I should work on is my concentration.

Like me, you will find you are stronger in some areas than others. Target your weakest areas for goal setting.

If you need to work on imagery then you will find Chapter 3 particularly helpful.

If you need to work on concentration then you will find Chapters 4 and 5 particularly helpful.

If you need to work emotional balance then you will find Chapters 5 and 6 particularly helpful.

The last questionnaire will give an idea of where you need to improve in the key areas of concentration, imagery and emotional balance. The other two important areas are fitness *(see Appendix I)* and technical skill *(see pages 5–9)*. These five areas cover all aspects of the game and setting goals in these areas will give you the physical and mental toughness you need to be a formidable competitor.

Now you need to pick the key qualities for best performance in your sport. The easiest way to do this is to pick a role model.

Think of athletes you admire – they may be world-class players or colleagues whom you admire and who play better than you do. What qualities do these models have in common?

You can also use yourself as a model when you play at your very best. What qualities do you have when you play at your best? They are likely to be the same as the qualities that you admire in the top athletes.

What qualities would you like to have on a more consistent basis?

If you wanted to play your best every time, what qualities would you need to work on?

These questions will suggest the key qualities that you need to work on.

Divide these qualities into the five main areas:

KEY QUALITIES

1	Fitness	What aspects of strength, speed or flexibility do you need to develop?
2	Technical skill	What parts of your game need work? Which parts let you down? Which aspects do you admire about your model and would like to work on for yourself?
3	Imagery	How do you want to improve your skills of imagery and mental rehearsal?
4	Concentration	How do you want to improve your powers of concentration?
5	Emotional balance	Do you want more will to win and emotional energy, or do you need less intensity and more ability to relax?

Think carefully about your key performance qualities. Fitness, concentration, emotional balance and technical skill are all qualities that you can work on directly. Imagery is slightly different because it helps all other aspects of your game.

Now you have all you need to make your performance profile:

■ knowledge of your present level of skills
■ a model of excellence to give you an idea of what to strive for
■ the key qualities you want to concentrate on

List these key qualities. Make them as specific as you can at this stage *(see the example below)*. Work with your coach if you have one.

The qualities will cover the three phases of your sport:

Before you play:	You need imagery and mental rehearsal, warm up, fitness exercise and preparation.
During the game:	You need technical skills and the ability to keep your concentration.
After the game:	Here you learn from what happened, what went well and what went wrong. In this phase, you also need to relax, take care of yourself and attend to any injuries.

Present State Score

In the first column put a score from one to ten to represent your present level of that quality.

Ten is the top score. If you are already playing at your top level, give yourself ten. (But if you are, then how can you set a goal to improve? This figure will always be less than ten.)

Desired State Score

In the next column write your desired level for each quality. Give this a score of ten out of ten in every case. Why try to be less than the best you can be?

In the third column, take the present state level from the desired state level and write down the difference.

In the fourth column rate how important you think this quality is to improving your game on a scale of one to ten. Not all qualities will be equal.

The fifth column will be your potential for improvement. This is the difference multiplied by the importance.

Here is an example of a fully completed performance questionnaire.

PERFORMANCE QUESTIONNAIRE (EXAMPLE)

Sport: Squash

Key Quality	Present Level	Desired Level	Difference	Importance	Potential
1 Fitness					
speed around the court	6	10	4	10	40
getting down to the ball	4	10	6	6	36
doing a good warm up	6	10	4	7	28
2 Technical Skill					
high backhand into the corners	5	10	5	4	20
back wall boast	3	10	7	2	14
drive from the back of the court	4	10	6	6	36
backhand cross-court drive	6	10	4	5	20

3 Imagery

clearer mental pictures	5	10	5	5	25
smoothness of mental rehearsal	6	10	4	3	12

4 Concentration

staying focused, ignoring distractions	6	10	4	10	40
staying focused when I lose several points in succession	4	10	6	8	48

5 Relaxation/Tension

more confident body language	4	10	6	6	36
more aggression	4	10	6	7	42

In this example the greatest potential for improvement is in:

staying focused when I lose several points in succession (concentration skill)	(48)
staying focused, ignoring distractions (concentration skill)	(40)
more confident body language (emotional balance skill)	(36)
more aggression (emotional balance skill)	(36)
getting down to the ball (fitness)	(36)

This process will give you a prioritized list of goals that are personal and relevant. They are yours, you will own them. You will avoid the trap of picking a goal because someone else has, or someone says you should, or they know someone for whom it worked well, etc.

There are two main types of goal: process goals and outcome goals.

- *Process goals* are about *how* you play. They need not involve others directly – for example, running a personal best time or increasing your stamina are both process goals. The performance questionnaire will have given you a series of prioritized process goals.

■   *Outcome goals* are about results – winning a match or a race.
     They can never be completely within your control, but you do
     everything in your power to get the right result, rather than hoping
     your adversary will make mistakes. Outcome goals involve other
     people.

When you have developed your process goals, it is much easier to set
some realistic and motivating outcome goals. Aim to work with
between four and seven goals at a time and make them a mixture of
outcome and process goals.

Now you have got the qualities that give *you* the most potential for
improvement. They may not have been obvious initially and will
probably include some that you have neglected because you did not
appreciate their importance or because they did not seem very interesting. Now you need to think about *how* to work on these goals to get the
best results.

The Seven Principles of Working with Goals

There are seven principles to bear in mind to make your goals realistic,
achievable and motivating. They apply to all goals – team and individual goals, outcome and process goals.

Principle 1: Say What You Want, Not What You Want
to Avoid

Goals have to be positive or they do not give you a desired state to
achieve. A goal is your destination and gives you a direction to move
towards. A positive goal tells you what to do. It sets out what you
want, for example, 'I will stay focused on the ball, whatever my opponent does.'
     Goals that are negative are like starting a journey by moving back-
wards or trying to win a game by stopping your opponent from winning.
A negative goal would be: 'I will not allow my opponent to distract me.'
The two sorts of goal look the same but the effect is different. Positive
goals are motivating and energizing. Negative goals are not.
     Unfortunately, thinking in negative terms sometimes seems more
sophisticated. 'I'm not too bad.' 'It's not a bad deal.' 'That's not a bad
idea.' Only a step up from this is the typically English expression that

damns with faint praise: 'It's quite nice.' This negative language is sometimes called 'exclusive language' because it excludes possibilities. But how much more powerful to say, 'I will win!' than 'I won't lose.' We have already seen from win–lose polar thinking how the 'I mustn't lose' mindset makes a loss more likely, not less. This is because the brain cannot deal with a negative in the same way as a positive. When you say to yourself, 'I mustn't lose,' what will you think about? Losing. 'I mustn't think of not losing' makes it even worse.

What you resist persists.

I once worked with a fine golfer who was not playing to his potential. His putting was excellent, but he had a problem teeing off when there was visible rough on either side of the fairway. He would invariably think to himself, 'I mustn't slice my shot into the rough, that would be a disaster.' Guess what often happened? He sliced into the rough. His brain made a picture and his hands made that picture come true. It didn't matter that the picture was *not* what he wanted. What mattered was that the picture was there drawing his attention like a hedgehog draws fleas and that influenced his body.

Words are powerful; they shape how we think. Start noticing all the times you use negative language – the times when you are thinking of what you do *not* want rather than what you *do* want and work out how you can change the thought so it expresses what you *do* want.

Exercise 7: Changing Negatives to Positives

During the next week, listen for ideas that are expressed in the negative. Notice when you and other people talk about what to avoid rather than what to achieve. Listen particularly when you are talking or thinking about sport.

Health Warning! When you hear others talk in negatives, do not jump in and correct them unless you are sure they are open to another way of thinking! Being too evangelistic about positive thinking usually only results in people thinking more negatively – about you.

Just notice your feelings when you hear negative language.

When you hear yourself being negative, correct yourself immediately. Do this silently or out loud (if appropriate). As you practise, you will start to catch the negative thought *before* you say it and change it to a positive if you want to.

Here are some examples of negative phrases and some positive equivalents:

Negative	Positive
'Not bad.'	'Good.'
'Can't complain.'	'I am satisfied.'
'I mustn't do this wrong.'	'I will do this right.'
'I mustn't lose.'	'I will win.'
'I hope this won't turn out badly.'	'I hope this will turn out well.'
'I can't see what more I can do.'	'I am content with what I have done.'
'I won't stop you.'	'I will help you.'
'Don't be tense!'	'Relax!'
'I don't have a problem with that.'	'That's a good idea.'
'It's not as bad as it seems...'	'It's as good as it seems...'
'Why don't we do that?'	'Let's do that!'
'That's not a bad idea.'	'That's a good idea.'
'Don't hit the ball out.'	'Keep the ball in.'
'Don't think in negatives.'	'Think in positives.'
'Don't worry...'	'Be assured...'

Occasionally the negative will be appropriate, but most of the time it is just an unhelpful way of thinking.

Key questions to ask if you have a negative goal:

> What do I want instead?
> What will that get for me?

Principle 2: Make Goals Challenging and Realistic

Make your goals attainable, but not too easy. Goals that are too easy are not motivating – although neither are goals that are too hard. More difficult goals will teach you more, so if you are unsure, err on the side of extra challenge because you do not know yet what you are capable of. Set your targets just out of reach – goals that you could not achieve if you were to carry on the way you have been.

Change your goals whenever necessary. The object is to succeed with a worthwhile goal, not to fail magnificently. When you achieve your goal, congratulate yourself and set the next one higher.

Constant small successes will keep you motivated. This reminds me of two courses I took at college. On one, we were given a big thick textbook and told that we would cover it all in the year. On the second course we were given a series of much smaller books and we moved from one to the next as we completed the work. My friends and I did much better in the latter course and enjoyed it more. It gave us a series of successes and 'chunked' the task in a way that made it more motivating. A ladder with a lot of small rungs is easier to climb than one with a few that are farther apart, especially if there is a big gap from the ground to the first rung.

One way to ensure that goals are realistic is to list all the difficulties that might stop you achieving your goal. Being aware of difficulties in advance makes them easier to deal with if they do arise. You can have a plan ready, or you can set other goals to deal with the difficulties. Also, you may look at your list of difficulties and blanch – they may be too much. Then you know that you have not set a realistic goal and you need to change it.

Key questions to ask:

Is this goal attainable?
Is this goal challenging?

Principle 3: Influence the Result Directly

A goal must be under your direct control. *You* must take action, not someone else, so when you plan what to do, all your plans should start with the phrase, 'I will...' followed by the action *you* will take. Your sporting achievements must come from your own efforts or your team effort. Others will certainly help you, but *you* will have to ask them.

There are two ways of talking about what we do and the words we use reflect how we think about it. The first is what is called 'the active voice'. This means *you* are the subject of the verb, *you* do something. For example, 'I won the race' or 'I set the goals', 'I ran three miles',

'I improved my backhand.' Notice the word 'I' is there in all the examples.

The second way of talking is 'the passive voice'. This puts the emphasis on *what* was done, for example, 'The race was won', 'The goals were set', 'Three miles were run', 'My backhand improved.' Nowhere does it say *who* did these things. The passive voice avoids responsibility, as in the famous government pronouncement: 'Mistakes were made.' No one is there in that phrase; it explains nothing.

We may use the passive voice because it is sometimes uncomfortable to take ownership of a goal (what if we fail?) or as a form of false modesty. Sometimes the passive voice is appropriate, but not when you are setting goals.

Listen carefully for how you phrase your goals to yourself and to others. When you use the passive voice you literally rub yourself off the mental picture. Make sure the word 'I' appears in all your goals.

Key questions:

Is this goal under my control?
What will I be doing to achieve this goal?

Principle 4: Measure your Progress

How will you measure your progress? There are various ways of doing this.

First, goals must be timed; you must give yourself a deadline. Either set a definite date, like the day of a competition, or give yourself a certain number of weeks to achieve what you want. A goal without a time frame is like a race without a finishing line – you cannot pace yourself.

Your goals should be a mixture of:

short-term goals (in the next month)
medium-term goals (one to six months)
long-term goals (six months and longer)

Secondly, you must decide how to measure your progress and how to continuously monitor it to make sure that you are on track.

Good goals are measurable. 'I want to be a better player' is a goal, but a very nebulous one. 'I want to get 85 per cent of my first serves in' is much better. Some measures are tangible. For example, goals can be measured in fixed times, weights or similar performance measures. For example, 'I am going to run the 1,500 metres in six minutes' or 'I am going to bench press 80 kg in future for three sets of ten' or 'I am going to convert 90 per cent of my drop kicks.' These measures are straight-forward and obvious. There will be no argument about whether you achieve these goals or not.

Sometimes you have to settle for less tangible measurements and rely on your own feelings, especially for goals like concentration and emotional balance. Sometimes these goals are not objectively quantifi-able – there is no accepted unit of concentration, kept in a sealed box in the Royal Society basement, because concentration is subjective. However, that does not mean you cannot measure it. You set up your own measurement, one that makes sense to you. You could set up a subjective measure on a scale of one to ten and measure your own per-formance. The previous performance questionnaire is an example of this. Your own feelings are a valuable measure as long as you are honest. The drawback is that they cannot be independently validated, like times and percentages.

You can measure in two ways, although many goals will have ele-ments of both methods:

1 *Relative to yourself.* Take the area you want to improve on, measure your present ability and set a goal to improve on that by a certain amount. 'I want to improve my goal average by 25 per cent this season' would be an example. This is the best way to measure improvement, because it starts from a realistic place – where you are now – and does not make comparisons with others. This is how process goals are measured.

2 *Relative to another person or team.* An example of this would be: 'I am going to beat Fred in the 1,500 metres next month.' To achieve this goal, you would not necessarily have to perform any better than you do already. You measure outcome goals this way.

Key questions:

When will I achieve this goal?
How do I measure this goal?
How will I know that I am achieving/have achieved this goal?

Principle 5: Check your Resources

What resources do you have to help you achieve your goal? Resources are anything or anyone who can help you. It is always more motivating to know that you have resources.

Make a list of the resources available to help you achieve your goals. Sometimes this list will turn out to be pleasantly lengthy, which is always reassuring. Resources may be books and magazines to give you ideas, sporting facilities, clubs and equipment. People are a resource – a coach particularly. Otherwise there will be friends, colleagues and teammates. There will also be role models you can use and great athletes who inspire you. Your own skills are resources – qualities like determination, concentration, imagery, commitment will help you. Goals are not isolated, they work together, and the qualities you have and improvements you make in one area may become resources for another area.

Key questions:

> What resources do I have?
> How can I get more help?

Principle 6: Count the Cost

You can have anything you want, the saying goes, providing you are willing to pay for it. What is the cost of your goals and are you willing and able to pay it? This is not simply cost in terms of money, but also in terms of time and the other things you could be doing if you were not working on your sports goals. Will your work suffer? Will you have time for your partner and family?

Sometimes it seems as though the way to achieve goals is to attack them single-mindedly and not be distracted by anything else. This temptation is strong for sports goals because they are so physical, they take time and physical effort. Make sure you keep your life in balance; it is possible to have too much of a good thing.

Think about other important people in your life and how they will be affected by these goals. A few months ago, a friend of mine was determined to improve his tennis. He set several challenging goals, took lessons from a professional, worked at his game and increased his ability to concentrate and his will to win. In short, he transformed his game in a few months. Before this he used to play socially at his local club with a group of friends and they would always have a few drinks afterwards. His tennis wasn't just sport, it was a social occasion. When he improved dramatically, he started beating all his tennis friends with monotonous regularity and these games were suddenly much less enjoyable for him (and them!) His friends suddenly started to make excuses that stopped them playing with him. My friend realized that his improvement had a cost that he had not anticipated. He lost his Saturday social games and it took him a little time to find other opponents who were at his level. Count the cost of your goal and decide if it is important enough to pursue.

Principle 7: Reward Yourself

Finally, you deserve a reward when you achieve a goal. Congratulate yourself. Treat yourself to some new sports equipment or whatever motivates you. Bask in the glow of self-satisfaction and other people's praise. You deserve it.

Action Plan

Now you need to set up a practice schedule and action plan to achieve your goals, otherwise you will be an armchair athlete.

First a warning about the word 'practice'. The word is usually taken to mean something you do to prepare for the 'real' performance. While this is true, you will not get the most out of your 'practice' sessions unless you act *as if* they are real and important. They may not be the actual match or race, but unless you enter into them wholeheartedly, you will not get the most benefit from them. How effective they are depends not just on the time you put in but on the quality of concentration, commitment and effort in that time. If you practise with less than 100 per cent commitment, then this will make it more difficult to raise your commitment in the real event. You have been practising giving less than you can. Whatever you practise you get better at doing. You do not want to get better at giving less than your best.

Also, in the heat of a match or competition, you become focused on results, on *what* you do, rather than how you do it. Your practice sessions are where you focus on *how* you perform, to build correct habits that will lift your game. You want your practice to ensure you cannot make a mistake.

Make up your schedule by listing your goals, writing your strategy beside them and then giving them a deadline. Leave space to monitor them at suitable intervals.

Here is an example of an action plan and practice schedule:

Action Plan

Goal 1 (Fitness): *To increase my stamina*

Measurement	The ability to play a squash match of five games without having to rest; the ability to chase down every ball in a rally
Priority	Top
Timing	Medium term
Strategy	Fifteen minutes three times a week of aerobic exercise; affirmations every day
Deadline	Three months

Goal 2 (Technical): *To improve my backhand straight drive*

Measurement	Getting 80 per cent of drives into the back corner
Priority	Secondary
Timing	Short term
Strategy	Two sessions a week of ten minutes driving the ball; three sessions a week of visualization mentally rehearsing the correct shot; reviewing videos of good players making the shot; affirmations every day
Deadline	Two months

Goal 3 (Mental): *To increase concentration*

Measurement	Subjective on a scale of one to ten, present value four
Priority	Top
Timing	Short/medium/long term
Strategy	Ten minutes three times a week of guided imagery performing against a distracting opponent; one session a week playing with a friend who will be deliberately distracting; affirmations to increase my concentration every day; post-match visualization session

| Deadline | Six months to increase measurement from four to seven |

Goal 4 (Balance): ***More confident body language***

Measurement	Subjective on a scale of one to ten – present level three; asking friends and spectators I know for feedback
Priority	Top
Timing	Short/medium term
Strategy	Mental rehearsal and visualization three times a week; listening to mental preparation audiotape the night before a match; affirmations; positive self-talk; keeping my head up at all times despite what happens in the match; post-match visualization session
Deadline	Three months

Goal 5 (Outcome): ***To play for the first team in my club***

Measurement	Obvious – to see my name on the board as selected and to play in the match
Priority	Medium
Timing	Medium term
Strategy	Working on previous four goals; coaching session every week; arranging friendly games with players already playing for the club
Deadline	Four months

Ink It – Think It – Say It

Goal setting needs practice. As you become more familiar with the technique, so your goals will become more focused. Make sure your action plan and practice schedule reflect your most important goals. Devote time to all three aspects of your game – fitness, technical skill and mental preparation. As you achieve your goals, make the next one more demanding, or add a new one to work on. Variety makes practice much more enjoyable.

Don't Just Think It – Ink It

Write each goal on a separate three inch by five inch card – not just any old scrap of paper, but good-quality clean card. Write your goals down in your best handwriting. Take them seriously. Your unconscious mind will react not so much to what you write, but how you write it. How impressed would you be with principles written on dirty scrappy paper that said how committed the writer was to them? Not much. Act committed even when no one else will see the goals.

Finally, make a short affirmation from each goal. An affirmation is a succinct statement of your goal that will deepen your commitment and keep your mind focused on it. You can also use these affirmations to motivate yourself during a match or race.

Affirmations can be powerful, but they have to be carefully phrased. When you make affirmations that are about self-development (process goals), phrase *them as if they are occurring now*. For example, if your goal were to increase your concentration in a match, a suitable affirmation would be: 'I am concentrating better and better, and I am focusing clearly on the game.' This makes it real-time and relevant. It has direction and energy.

Avoid the two common mistakes that people make with affirmations. First, do not phrase them as if they have already happened. For example, 'I have tremendous focus and concentration.' If it is not true at that moment, another part of your mind will say, 'Oh no you haven't. Who are you trying to kid?'

The second mistake is to give these self-development affirmations an exact deadline as if they will be magically achieved when the clock strikes the hour, for example, 'In three months' time I shall be more focused and better able to concentrate.' Then the deeper part of your mind will reply, 'Oh, fine. I needn't do anything now then.' Only outcome goals should have such exact deadlines. Affirmations should have a specific time and date only if they are about specific actions and you want to prepare yourself, for example, 'On Wednesday 1 July, I will get up at 6 a.m. and run five miles as part of my training.'

Write your affirmations on good-quality paper and say them to yourself every day. When you achieve the goal, fold up the paper and file it away under 'Success Stories' before writing a new affirmation.

Beliefs

Do you believe in yourself? Do you believe you can achieve your goals? Are any beliefs stopping you from achieving what you are capable of achieving?

You need to believe three things about your goals:

Possibility: They are possible to achieve.
Ability: You are capable of achieving them.
Worthiness: You deserve to achieve them.

Possibility, **A**bility and **W**orthiness are the three keys to achievement. Remember them as 'the PAW Process'.

Possibility

We all have physical limits because we are human and not superheroes. We are limited by upbringing, body type and sometimes just plain bad luck. But – *we do not usually know what these limits are. You cannot know what they are until you reach them.* Once it was considered impossible for any human being to run a mile in less than four minutes – until Roger Bannister did it at Oxford on 6 May 1954. Then another runner bettered that time shortly afterwards and it was suddenly as if a mental block had been lifted from the world's athletes. More and more athletes ran a four-minute mile. It became commonplace. Around the same time two other 'impossible' records were broken. Parry O'Brien put the shot past the 60-foot marker and Charles Dumas cleared 7 foot in the high jump.

Do not be too quick to decide what is impossible.

Ability

Have you put a mental ceiling on your achievements? If you have seen the film *Indiana Jones and the Temple of Doom* you will remember the scene where our intrepid archaeologist hero is trapped in a cave beneath the Maharaja's palace. The door has slammed shut and his companion leans on a lever that starts a spiky ceiling moving downwards. Down and down it moves inexorably. Soon our hero will be impaled on the spikes and then crushed.

We all have a mental ceiling on our achievements. It is not real and it is usually set too low. It may seem to move down inexorably with advancing age. We may be cramped by a self-imposed mental ceiling. This can be particularly true when we think of what we are capable of physically. Try this next exercise to push up the ceiling.

Exercise 8: Your Sports Ceiling – Escaping the Temple of Doom

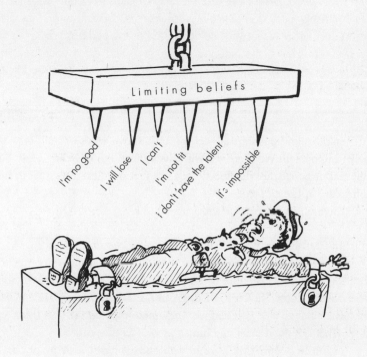

Figure 2.1: The Temple of Doom

Imagine yourself in a room that represents your sporting potential. Look around you. How big is it? You may find that it is as big as the area you play your sport on – for example, a golf green, a tennis court or football field. Take a look around. Is it big enough for you?

Change it as you wish, for example, make it bigger, add some colour, perhaps add some cheering spectators.

Now look up.

Imagine a ceiling above you that represents the limit of what you think you can achieve.

How far away is it?
What does it look like?
What sort of colour is it?
Put up your hands and feel it.
Feel the shape and texture of it under your hands.
Now push it far upwards. Hear a grinding or a clanking of gears as you do so. Watch it move upwards and disappear.

Now you have a more realistic way of thinking about your sporting achievements – you do not know what you are capable of and therefore you do not know where your ceiling is. One day perhaps you will come up against it, but in the meantime you can stand up to your full height and enjoy the feeling that there is one less self-imposed barrier limiting your success.

Affirmations and pushing the ceiling up are two ways of building your belief in yourself. We often sell ourselves short by not believing in ourselves. But beliefs are not facts, they are just our best guess about how things are at the moment.

Have one basic true belief:

You have not yet reached the limit of what you are capable of.

You know you are capable of something when you do it. Until then, you do not know, so keep an open mind. For the same reason, it is important not to say you cannot do something, even if you think you can't. This is a good principle in life as well as in sport.

Listen to people talk around you and you will hear more admissions of 'can't' than 'can'. People will own up much more readily to what they are bad at than what they are good at, perhaps because they think admitting they are good is boastful hubris. And they might have to prove it. Suppose they fail? It is a great burden to be a top athlete within your circle (and that circle may be the local league, or, if you are Pete Sampras, the world) – you have everything to lose and nowhere to go but down. Like the legendary gunslingers in the old Wild West, every young pretender is out for your crown. But whatever your level, don't say things like:

'I can't hole a putt from more than 6 feet away.'

'I can't hit a decent backhand passing shot.'
'I am not good at saving penalties.'

This sort of talk just wraps a straitjacket of imposed limitations ever tighter by getting others to agree with you. If you find yourself thinking like this, then add the little word 'yet' to the end of the sentence.

There is no need to boast, but no need to talk yourself down either.

Worthiness

Do you deserve to achieve your goals? Only you can answer this question, but why not? Sporting achievement is straightforward and not tangled in moral principles. Unless you have taken drugs or bribed your opponents, you deserve to win.

Say to yourself 'I deserve to achieve my goals' and notice how comfortable you feel. If you feel uncomfortable, what would you have to do to feel comfortable?

Put your goals through the PAW questions. Say for each goal:

'This goal is possible.'
'I have the ability to achieve this goal.'
'I deserve to achieve this goal.'

Notice any uncomfortable feelings. They will point to obstacles and self-doubts. The next exercise will help you with these.

Exercise 9: Obstacle Course

Go through your goals and think of reasons why you might not achieve them. Begin by saying to yourself, just as an experiment, 'I will not achieve my goal because...' and then list all the possible reasons that come into your mind. If you are really having trouble achieving a goal, list all the reasons why you think this is so.

You may think of many reasons, for example, you are not strong enough, ambitious enough, or you do not have the opportunity. These objections will fall into one of four categories that are referred to as the *neurological levels* in NLP. The American trainer and researcher Robert Dilts originally developed these and I have amended them slightly.

1 The first neurological level is the *environment*. The environment is the where, the when and the people and things involved. Objections on this level might be: 'I do not have the equipment, I do not have the right coach, the right people to support me, I'm too old/young/not the right age...'

2 The second level is what you do – your *behaviour and skills*. Objections at this level would be: 'I don't have the sporting skills or the right ways of thinking' (because thinking is a skill too).

3 The third level is *beliefs and values*. An objection here would be that a goal was not important enough for you to bother spending time and effort on. If a sporting goal is not important enough to you, or the cost (as you perceive it) is too great, then you won't do it, so don't try to force yourself. To force behaviour (achieving a sporting goal) in the face of an objection at the values level is asking for trouble. You will not feel comfortable and will find many other reasons to fail.

4 The fourth level is *identity*. This is your perception of yourself – who you are. An objection at this level would be: 'I'm not the sort of person to do that.' This is a perfectly reasonable objection and if you feel this way, just drop the goal.

Summary of objections:

1 You don't have the resources – the people, equipment, time and place.
2 You have the resources, but you don't know what to do.
3 You know what to do, but you do not have the skill.
4 You have the skill, but it doesn't seem worth it.
5 It is worthwhile, but somehow it's 'just not you'.

Once you have your list of objections, how many of them are real obstacles and how many of them are your beliefs?

At this stage there are three possibilities:

1 Your objections are real tangible obstacles that make it impossible for you to achieve your goals.
2 They are real obstacles that you could get around if you devoted the time and effort to doing so.

3   They are beliefs about yourself or other people. You do not really
    know for sure whether they are true, but they are your best guess at
    the moment.

In the first case, just drop the goal. It's a waste of time to pursue it.

In the second case you have to decide whether you really want the
goal enough to put in the time and effort. If you do, put in the time and
effort. If you do not, acknowledge that, and let the goal go.

In the third case, think how you might test whether that belief is true
or not. In other words, does the obstacle really exist outside your head?
How real is it? Beliefs can be very effective obstacles, but only when we
think they are true. Once you know whether your belief is true or not,
then the obstacle will fall into the first or second case above.

This approach will give you responsibility for your goals. You can
reclaim the power that you have given to other people and circumstances to stop you. That means that you can never blame anyone else
or any set of circumstances for not achieving your goals. You will be
much more clear and focused on your goals and actions. You decide.
You are responsible.

Keep track of your goals. Review them regularly. Reward yourself when
you achieve them and enjoy those moments. Sporting triumphs can be
fleeting. Many top sportsmen and women have regretted that after all
the long hours of training and practice, all the emotional turmoil of
competition, they were too exhausted or consumed by false modesty or
dazed to really appreciate the moment of triumph. Enjoy it! It's what
you have worked for and you deserve it. Collect those moments – put
beautiful pictures in a photograph album or press cuttings in a scrap-
book. Go back to them. Use them to motivate yourself in the future. All
our memories can be a rich source of inspiration, learning and pleasure
for the rest of our lives, providing we are actually there in the moment
to experience them. How we can do this is the main subject of the next
chapter.

REFERENCES

Gould, D., Tammen, V., Murphey, S., and May, J., 'An examination of
    US Olympic sports psychology consultants and the services they
    provide', *The Sport Psychologist* 3 (1989), 300–12

Weinburg, R.S., Stitcher, T., and Richardson, P., 'Effects of seasonal goal setting program on lacrosse performance', *The Sport Psychologist* 8 (1994), 166–75

CHAPTER TWO SUMMARY

Goals are what you want to achieve.

They give you a sense of purpose.
They motivate you.
They give you something against which to measure your performance.
They give you a focus in your sport.

Goals should be motivating, realistic, achievable and challenging.

Make a performance profile that will help you set a good programme of goals to achieve. You will need:

- knowledge of your present level of skills
- a model of excellence so you know what to strive for
- the key qualities you want to concentrate on in your goal-setting programme

First decide the key qualities that contribute to the best performance in your sport.
Use a role model – either an athlete you admire or yourself when you are playing at your best. Set goals based on those qualities.
Distribute your goals between these areas:

- imagery
- concentration
- emotional balance
- technical skill
- fitness

Take the key qualities and work out your potential for improvement with the Performance questionnaire *(see page 33)*.
Prioritize your goals.
Work with between four and seven goals at a time.

Make your goals a mixture of:

- short-term goals (in the next month)
- medium-term goals (one to six months)
- long-term goals (six months and longer)

Goals may be:

Process goals: about how you play (measured relative to yourself)
Outcome goals: about results (measured relative to others)

The seven principles of working with goals are:

1 Say what you want, not what you want to avoid.
2 Make goals challenging and realistic.
3 Influence the result directly.
4 Measure your progress.
    You can measure goals in two ways:
    relative to yourself
    relative to another person or team.
5 Check your resources.
6 Count the cost.
7 Reward yourself.

Draw up an action plan and a practice schedule.
    Write down your goals.
    Write an affirmation for each goal.
    When you write self-development affirmations, phrase them
        as if they are occurring now.
    When you write affirmations of objective achievements,
        phrase them with a definite deadline.
    You need to believe that:

- The goals are possible to achieve. (We do not know what is possible until we attempt it.)
- You are capable of achieving them. (We often place too low a ceiling on our capabilities.)
- You deserve to achieve them.

Identify any beliefs that might be holding you back by identifying obstacles at the different neurological levels:

- environment
- behaviour and skills
- beliefs and values
- identity

These obstacles may be:

- real and insurmountable
- real but surmountable with help
- beliefs subject to being proven wrong

Test the third category and assign all goals to one of the first two categories.

Track your goals and fully enjoy the times when you achieve them.

Imagery: The Power
of the Imagination

Just Imagine. . .

You are in one of your favourite places – perhaps on holiday, maybe in a forest, on a beach or in a favourite room. Get inside your mental picture, take a look around. What do you see? How easily can you imagine your surroundings?

Now imagine a friend talking or imagine you are listening to some of your favourite music. How easily do you hear that in your mind?

Now imagine reaching out and touching something. Imagine you can smell some wonderful dish cooking and then imagine raising some of that food to your lips. . .

Just as we can see, hear, taste, touch and smell the outside world, so we can re-create those same sensations in our mind. We reach out and experience the outside world through our senses, and when we think, we reach in and re-experience or re-present the world to ourselves through using our senses inwardly. Either we remember our experience or imagine it – I can equally well picture myself running for a bus (which I have done), as winning the 100 metres dash at the Olympic Games (which I have not).

When we use our senses inwardly to think they are known as *representational systems* in NLP literature. You think using the representational systems of sight, hearing, feeling (including the sense of balance and sense of touch), taste and smell. We use these representational systems to plan everything we do and we will use them for mental rehearsal to improve our sports skills. Most mental rehearsal is random and unfocused, more like daydreaming. Mental rehearsal is a powerful technique and when we know how we think, we can hone it to be more powerful still.

Mental rehearsal uses the power of your imagination – the strongest power you have. Will-power needs emotion and emotion comes from our ability to imagine what we want, what is important to us and what inspires us. Will-power cannot work alone, it runs on emotional energy. Using your will-power alone is like pushing a car up a hill when you could be driving it. Your imagination provides the fuel. If will-power were enough to achieve goals, then people would be able to give up smoking, keep New Year's resolutions, easily stay at their ideal weight and never lose their temper (unless they wanted to). Pit the imagination against the will and the imagination will win every time.

Your imagination dominates your will.

Remember my golfer friend who would slice the ball into the trees? He did not want to. He used his will-power not to. But he still mentally rehearsed mishitting the ball. His imagination went to the trees and the ball followed shortly afterwards. Harness this power to work *for* you or it may work *against* you, whispering in your ear, distracting you, suddenly popping up mental pictures of what you don't want. And your muscles will follow your imagination because every movement starts with an idea.

Imagine walking along a path about 3 feet wide. Easy. Now imagine that same path along the side of a mountain with a sheer rock face on one side and a drop of 1,000 feet on the other. Don't look down! Now how easy is it to walk the path? But the path is the same, only your way of thinking about it has changed. Stay with the fantasy but shift your perspective again. When you look down, imagine what you see are small objects that are close to you and not large objects that are 1,000 feet away. Now they are so near you could reach out and touch them. And you can walk easily again.

Sport involves your body and mind, so mental preparation for sport involves all the internal senses. The more vividly you can use your representational systems, the more focused and effective your mental rehearsal will be. Visualization means seeing mental pictures. Imagery means using any representational system. It means imagining clear images, sounds and feelings, perhaps smells and tastes.

Imagery is one of the most powerful and versatile tools for an athlete to use. You can use it to mentally rehearse technical skills, to control pre-match nerves and to relax after the game. You can use imagery to prepare you for pressure so that you can keep your concentration in a match. Sport can put you under intense mental pressure –

equal to a cliff walk! Imagine what it would be like to take part in a penalty shoot out at the end of a World Cup match. Millions of people are watching. Your country's chances depend on you keeping your nerve. If you score, everyone breathes a sigh of relief and tenses up for the next shot. The road to fame is not to score but to miss. Remember the penalty shoot out between England and Germany in the Euro '96 Tournament? Who do you remember? The players who scored, or Gareth Southgate, the player who missed? Even in a situation where the eyes of the world are not fixed on you, the eyes of your friends, spouse, teammates and reporters from the local newspaper can still put you under a lot of pressure. Mental rehearsal is the only way of preparing for this.

The Uses of Sports Imagery

Imagery can be used for:

- improving a technical skill (for example, imagining doing perfect penalty goal kicks)
- counteracting negative images of mistakes, lost points, near misses, etc.
- relaxation before a match and controlling pre-match nerves (for example calming your nerves by imagining relaxing on a beach)
- getting more energy and confidence before a game (for example, imagining making the winning shot, hearing the applause of the crowd in your mind)
- working out tactics and problem solving before the game (for example, how you will deploy the team on the field)
- general preparation when you are unsure of conditions in advance (for example, imagining competing in difficult or unusual conditions)
- calming yourself when you become tense during a match (for example, imagining the referee with purple hair and a clown's mask when he gives a poor decision against you)
- learning from your game afterwards (for example, replaying critical points of the game afterwards in your mind to see if there was anything you could have done differently)

> ■ healing sports injuries (for example using suggestions and
>   relaxation to speed the healing of a pulled ligament in
>   conjunction with medical treatment and physiotherapy)

How Imagery Works

How does imagery work? There seems to be a huge difference between
doing something and 'just' thinking about it.

Try this experiment. Imagine holding a big juicy lemon. Feel it in
your hand. Imagine smelling it. Now imagine taking a knife and cut-
ting it in half. Pick up one half and smell the cut flesh. Bring it up to
your mouth and get ready to take a bite (or maybe if you want, lick it
first). Are you starting to salivate? (I am as I write this description!) The
lemon is imaginary, but the saliva is real.

Every action begins as a thought and we can make real physical
changes just by thinking, because our body responds to our thoughts.
Our mind is like a virtual reality machine – what we think about is
real and when we are asleep our mind's creations become dreams that
take on a reality that seems completely compelling because our connection to the outside world and guardian of reason, our conscious
mind, is off duty.

Here is another interesting experiment. Make a pendulum using a
piece of thin thread, about a foot long, with a small weight tied on
the end. Hold it so that gravity makes it hang straight down. Notice
the small random movements it makes as it swings, responding to the
small muscle movements in your hand. Now imagine that it is starting
to swing clockwise. Do not actually try to make it swing clockwise, but
just imagine it is. Close your eyes for half a minute while you picture
the pendulum rotating clockwise. What happens? You may be surprised when you open your eyes that the pendulum actually has
started to swing clockwise (unless you are so resistant to it swinging
clockwise that you tense the muscles in your arm. Then it is likely to
swing anti-clockwise.)

Your thoughts affect your muscles directly. Imagine the consequences of this when you are in the middle of a game and you start to
think you are going to lose. That thought will affect your muscles and
unless you counteract the thought it will come true.

Mental rehearsal works because we can use our thoughts to pro-gramme our muscles. Mental imagery mimics real physical rehearsal, provides a blueprint for success and gives confidence. When you have done something already several times in your mind, it is no longer new and unknown, but feels familiar. When we imagine an action, micro-muscle movements mimic the muscle activity that would take place if we actually made that movement.

You can mentally practise anything beforehand. And practice, as they say, makes perfect (provided it is prefect practice). There is a limit to how long you can practise for real without tiring. But you can prac-tise mentally for much longer.

There is a great deal of research to back up these claims for mental rehearsal. Richard Suinn, a professor at Colorado State University, has trained Olympic athletes using a method he called visio-motor behavior rehearsal (VMBR). Athletes went through a stage of mental and physical relaxation and then mentally rehearsed the movements they wanted to make in the sport. Suinn measured the muscle activity in the legs of skiers as they imagined a downhill run with electromyographic (EMG) readings. He found that the electrical patterns in the muscles were very close to those that would have occurred if these men had been skiing for real. There was even a final burst of muscle activity as the subjects imagined themselves passing the finishing line and slowing themselves down.

In John Lane's study of imagery and sport in 1980, two groups of equally skilled amateur athletes were asked to practise shooting free throws in basketball for 20 minutes a day for two weeks. One group supplemented this with relaxation and imagery. When both groups were tested, both had improved; however the group who had used imagery had improved 11 to 15 per cent more than the players who had not used imagery.

A study by Barbara Kolonay in 1977 also used free throws in bas-ketball. In this study a group that used imagery and relaxation improved more than two other groups, one that used imagery alone and one that used relaxation alone. So relaxation seems to make imagery more effective still. It makes it easier and it counteracts any muscle tension that might get in the way of the micro-muscle move-ments that are the basis of mental rehearsal.

What might stop you using imagery? Some people claim that they do not make any mental images at all. When they close their eyes all they 'see' is a blank. This is their experience, but everyone must make mental images somehow, otherwise how would they recognize their house or their car, how would they know their friends from strangers? When you see someone approaching in the street, you know if you have met them before because you have stored mental images of the people you know. You are not aware of storing these images at the time, it happens so fast, but they have to be there.

To make the most of imagery you need to:

- be aware of the pictures
- make them as vivid as possible
- vary the perspective from which you see them
- be able to control them

This will help you not only in sport but also in any other situation where you want to use imagery to achieve your goals.

Imagery uses all the senses, not just the ability to see mental pictures. The next three exercises are designed to develop and improve your imagery skills for effective mental rehearsal. Make notes as you go through of which ones you find the easiest. For example, you may find it easy to see mental pictures but harder to hear sounds. Or perhaps sounds are easy, but not feelings of balance. Do these exercises in a place where you can relax and you will not be disturbed.

Exercise 10: Preparing Imagery – Pictures

Close your eyes, relax your body and watch your mental screen. Describe what you see to yourself. It will be shades of grey with splashes of white at first. You may see a negative image of what you had been looking at before. When this settles down, imagine a small black speck in the centre of your visual field. Make it as black as you can. Now imagine that speck growing like ink dropped into a pool of water so that it slowly spreads out from the centre and starts to colour your entire mental screen. The blacker you can get the screen, the better. Put your hand over your eyes if this helps.

Now open your eyes and look at an object near you. Relax your eyes, don't stare at it or 'try' to imprint it on your mind. Gradually close your eyes. As you do, try to keep a picture of it in your mental field of vision. It may help to look up to your left, even though your eyes are closed. The position of your eyes helps you to think in certain ways and looking up or defocusing makes visualization easier. Close your eyes and imagine the object in front of you exactly how it was.

What colour was the object?

See the colour as vividly as you can.

Now see if you can make your picture even brighter.

Imagine a spotlight on the object making it stand out more clearly.

Imagine making the object smaller so it recedes into the distance. Now make it zoom up close.

Perspective is important in mental rehearsal. You need to be able to control your picture by controlling the angle you see it from.

Imagine yourself floating on the ceiling looking down on the object.

Now imagine yourself on the floor looking up at the object.

Now move the object in your mind. Imagine turning it upside-down so you can see it from the bottom.

Then turn it around so you can see it from the back.

If this is difficult, open your eyes and do it to the object (if you can), then close your eyes and visualize what you have just seen.

Imagine turning the object inside-out and looking at it from the inside.

Now imagine clambering inside it so you can look at it from the inside.

Some books on visualization give the impression that everyone can see amazing three-dimensional vivid pictures that stay imprinted on their mind for minutes at a time and anything less is not good enough. This is not true. People vary a great deal as to how easily and vividly they visualize, but everyone can improve the clarity of the images and the degree of control they have over them by practising. Everyone has a photographic memory, only some people have better-quality film in their camera. Mental rehearsal will work however well you visualize, but the better you visualize, the more effective it will be.

Exercise 11: Preparing Imagery – Associated and Dissociated

Close your eyes and imagine floating up towards the ceiling. Imagine the ceiling getting closer and closer. Now imagine looking down from your new vantage point.

Now imagine floating down again, seeing the bed or chair get closer and closer until you are back where you started. When you are inside your body, seeing pictures through your own eyes, then you are *associated*.

Now imagine floating out of your body, seeing your body sitting in the chair. See it from different angles, imagine you can go 'astral travelling' through the room, seeing your body from different viewpoints. Now float back down again. Your body hasn't left the chair, yet it seems as though you have. When you see yourself as if from the outside, you are *dissociated*.

When you are associated, you are in the experience. When you are dissociated, you are outside it. Being associated is like being in the thick of the game, being dissociated is like seeing the same game from the substitutes' bench.

This difference is very important. Associated imagery practice has very different effects from dissociated practice. When you are associated, you experience the feelings that go with the mental picture. Try this experiment:

Think of a pleasant memory.
When you think back to it, check what sort of picture you have in your mind.
Are you associated, seeing out through you own eyes?
Are you dissociated, seeing yourself in the situation?
Whichever it is, change it and try the other way.
Now change it back to what it was.
Which way do you prefer?

For most people, being associated brings back the feeling more strongly because they are inside their body and so more in touch with their feelings.

When you are dissociated, you are out of touch with your body. You will still have feelings, but they will be *about* what you see and will not be the same as the feelings when you are inside the experience. Dissociation is a useful technique if you want to put some distance between you and a memory. As a general rule, think of your pleasant memories in an associated way to get the most enjoyment from them and your uncomfortable memories in a dissociated way to avoid the bad feelings.

Association and dissociation describe not only ways of seeing a mental picture but also ways of experiencing. Some days you feel 'all there', really in your body – you want to engage in the moment and have fun, you are associated. Other days you may feel 'out of touch' or reflective, more like an observer as life passes by – you are dissociated.

When you are playing your sport you should be fully associated in the present moment. Dissociation is best for planning, analysing and learning from experience.

We have many phrases that bring out the difference between the association and dissociation.

Ways of Talking about Association and Dissociation

Associated	Dissociated
in the experience	out of it
all there	laid back
living in the thick of it	on the sidelines
with it	not with it
caught up	not all there
in the flow	not quite yourself
in touch	out of touch

Exercise 12: Preparing Imagery – Sounds

Close your eyes for this exercise. Clap your hands. Hear that sound again in your mind. Now imagine that same sound again, first louder, then softer. Clap your hands again if you have difficulty remembering it.

Now imagine the sound coming from across the room. Then imagine it from above you, now from below you. It may help if you *imagine* clapping your hands again.

Now imagine the sound of the voice of someone in your immediate family. Hear them say something. It may help if you make an image of them and see them opening their mouth and speaking. It may help if you look across to the side. This eye position makes it easier to hear internal sounds.

Next, imagine some of your favourite music, just a few bars. Make it louder, then softer. Make it faster, then slower. Make it come from different parts of the room.

There are two strategies that may help you hear sounds more clearly in your mind. First, visualize the sound being made. For example, see someone strumming a guitar, blowing a trumpet or hitting the drums. As you see that, the sound will come naturally. This strategy works well if you are good at making mental pictures.

Secondly, you could imagine yourself playing the instrument. It does not matter whether you really can or not. Be associated and imagine strumming the guitar, blowing the trumpet or hitting the drum. Hear the sounds as you do so. This strategy works well if you find it easy to imagine feelings.

Exercise 13: Preparing Imagery – Feelings, Tastes and Smells

This exercise is also best done with your eyes closed.

Touch your arm lightly, then imagine your finger touching your arm and re-create that same feeling.

Now move your arm into the air and then put it back down. Now re-create that feeling without moving your arm. See your arm move up in your imagination and get the feeling at the same time.

Imagine standing up, walking to the other end of the room, turning around, walking back and sitting down again. It may help to look down to your right as you do this. Looking down helps you get in touch with your feelings.

Now imagine yourself sitting down to one of your favourite meals. Smell the aroma of the food. See the food on the plate in front of you. Now imagine lifting some towards your mouth. Feel the texture of the food in your mouth, imagine chewing it and then swallowing. How real an experience can you make that?

These exercises give you a strong basis on which to develop your imagery skills.

Preferred Ways of Thinking

Which of these exercises did you find easy? Which took the most effort? We all use all the representational systems, but tend to favour one, our preferred way of thinking. Some people use a lot of mental imagery. They make detailed pictures of their plans, hopes and dreams. People who are good at visualization often show a talent for drawing, art or architecture, sometimes mathematics or design work. For other people, thinking means talking to themselves. They may be very good with words and are often teachers, lecturers, writers or trainers. Others who can discriminate between many different sorts of sounds are likely to be good at music. There are those who think more with their body than with their head; they are often more intuitive and go by their feelings. Good athletes often have this natural body sensitivity. No one teaches us how to think – we tend to go with what comes naturally, or what our parents favour.

We not only think with our head but with our bodies too. We move our bodies naturally in certain ways to help us think. Typically people will look up or defocus their eyes when they are visualizing, look across to the left or right when they are hearing sounds internally and look down to their right when they are thinking kinesthetically. They will usually look down to their left when talking to themselves. It is very interesting to watch other people's eye movements, especially on television, and listen to the words they use that may match their way of thinking. (It is not a good idea to try to follow your own eye movements! They do not need your attention and work best without it.) How many times have you seen someone stare into the distance and say, 'Let me see?' You will see people look down when they are in the grip of an emotion, we even say a person is 'down' if they are depressed. Our body language always links with our thinking. You cannot tell *what* a person is thinking, but you can nearly always tell *the way they are thinking it.*

Moving your eyes in the natural ways that link with different thinking styles will help your imagery. It also helps if you move your head and not just your eyes when you make these movements. Defocus or look up when you want to visualize. Look to either to the left or right if you want to hear sounds internally and down to your right if you want to get in touch with bodily feelings. Look down to your left if you want to talk to yourself. *(See Appendix II for a summary of these eye movements.)*

It makes sense to develop all the ways of thinking to give your thinking the greatest amount of flexibility and richness. Do you know the way of thinking you prefer? You can easily find out.

Exercise 14: Discovering your Preferred Way of Thinking

We use all the ways of thinking, just as we use all our senses, but we usually pay attention to one sense at a time, so we will pay most attention to one representational system. We develop our senses on the outside to become sensitive and attentive, so we develop our representational systems on the inside to become clearer thinkers.

Notice your thoughts as you go through the day, particularly if you have to deal with problems. Do you tend to make a lot of pictures? Do you hear sounds or talk to yourself? Are you mostly aware of your feelings? This will give you a clue.

A good way you can find out your preferred way of thinking is to write freely for a few minutes about the events of the day, or about your work, or your last match or race, about what you liked and what you did not like. Say the thoughts aloud to a tape recorder if you prefer (this in itself is a clue that you might prefer the auditory system). Then review what you wrote or recorded. How many words refer to seeing, for example 'look', 'picture', 'horizon', 'focus', 'scene', any sort of colour or show? These are visual words, words that imply seeing something. How many words did you use that have to do with the sense of hearing, for example 'say', 'discuss', 'proclaim', 'remark', 'listen', 'tell', 'silence', 'harmony'? These words imply hearing. Finally, how many feeling words did you use about the sense of touch and balance, for example 'touch', 'handle', 'contact', 'push', 'rub', 'hold', 'grasp' and 'solid'?

Sensory words like these are known as *predicates* in NLP. We use them to describe the outside world in terms of what we see, hear and feel, and we also use them to describe what we see, hear and feel in our mental world. Many words we use are neutral and do not imply any way of thinking. There are some examples of predicates and common phrases using sensory words in Appendix II.

Knowing your preferred way of thinking makes imagery easier. Begin the imagery from whichever representational system is easiest to access. For example, if you find visualization easy, start with a mental picture and then see if you can add the sounds and feelings. If you find feelings easiest, then start with the feeling and then construct the image by adding pictures and sounds. Always start from your strength and then move on to the others.

Once you are sensitive to predicates you will also start to notice how people describe events in ways that imply different ways of thinking. For example, three friends go to a football match. The first says, 'It was a *brilliant* game! I'll give you the *highlights*. Both teams played really well, we had a grandstand *view* and the *lighting* was good. We *saw* our team home by three goals to two. I'll *watch* it on television again tonight.' The second says, 'What a great match! Let me *tell* you about it. The atmosphere was fantastic, everyone was *yelling* support and I couldn't *hear* myself think. I *shouted* myself hoarse. I *listened* to the commentary on my Walkman and that was good too.' The third says, 'It was a *knockout* game! The first half was *hard*, but in the end, our team won *comfortably*, the other team never really *got into* the game in the second half. The seats weren't very *comfortable* though. I'll *catch* it on television tonight.' These are exaggerated examples, but you can see the first example uses many visual predicates, the second many auditory ones and the third many feeling or kinesthetic ones. When you watch sport on television you will hear a lot of kinesthetic predicates, and you will also be able to tell a lot about the preferred thinking style of the commentator by watching their eye movements and body language and listening to their predicates.

Ask what happened at a party, to take another example, and some people will be able to recount what everyone was wearing, the colours and the styles, others will tell you all the music that was played and others were just dancing!

The Critical Qualities of Imagery

Now you are almost ready to design the most effective imagery programme for yourself using the three main representational systems – seeing (visual), hearing (auditory) and feeling (kinesthetic).

Your pictures, sounds and feelings have certain qualities. For example, your pictures will have a certain brightness and colour, sounds a certain rhythm and tone, and feelings a certain texture and temperature. These qualities are known in NLP as *submodalities*. The senses are the *modalities* we use to think, so the qualities of the sense experience are the *submodalities*. The *critical submodalities* are those qualities that will make the imagery most effective for you.

Exercise 15: Finding your Critical Submodalities for Mental Rehearsal

Think of a time when you played or competed very well. You felt great about your performance, whether you won or not.

Visual Submodalities

Create a mental picture of that time. If you do not see a picture, pretend you have a picture. If you did, what would it be like? You will have a glimpse and that is enough. (There must be some picture, or you would not be able to think of that exact time.)

Are you looking out through your own eyes (associated) or do you see yourself in the picture (dissociated)?

If you are not associated already, step into the picture and associate. You need to associate in your mental rehearsal imagery for the best results.

Scan your picture.

How big is it?
How far away does it seem to be?
Is it moving or still?
Does the picture have colours? If so, how intense are they?
Is it moving? If so, how fast are the movements?
Whereabouts do you see it in your visual field (for example, up, down to the left or right)?
How wide is your visual field?
How clearly focused is the picture?
Is there anything else about the picture that seems important to you?

Pretend you are a film producer. Your job is to make the most satisfying, clear and exciting movie possible for your audience. You are the hero of the movie and you are the audience. You only have to please yourself. You can play with all the submodalities. Get the best colour, the right camera angle and the right speed. Experiment with changing all the qualities of the picture – for example, make the picture bigger, then smaller. Which is the best? Which makes the film the most real and intense? Try moving the picture closer, then farther away, experiment with the camera angle until you have a picture that you enjoy and is real and intense for you. You are the hero of this film, too, so make it a good one!

Make notes of any submodalities that have a big impact on your movie. These show how you encode your thoughts. You want to make sure that you clothe your mental rehearsal in the submodalities that represent successful, enjoyable, satisfying play for *you*. For someone else they may be different, which is why an 'off the shelf' imagery programme is not so effective. There is an example of one athlete's submodality worksheet at the end of this exercise.

Auditory Submodalities

Now review your movie, because we are going to add a soundtrack.

Are there any sounds or words in it?
If so, whereabouts do they come from?
How far away are they?

What sort of rhythm do they have?
How loud are they?
How long do they last?
Is there internal dialogue? If so, what is it saying?
Any other aspects of the sounds that seems important to you?

Explore the auditory submodalities in the same way that you explored the visual ones. Experiment with changing them and make a note of what gives you the most satisfying soundtrack.

Kinesthetic Submodalities

Finally, you want to feel this movie.

First separate the feelings *about* the movie from the feelings *of* the movie. For example, you may feel proud and triumphant at the memory of the event. This is good, but when you are inside the memory, you also want the feelings of the experience, especially the bodily feelings of touch and balance.

What sort of feelings do you have when you are inside the memory?
Where do you feel them?
How intense are they?
How warm or cold are they?
What shape do you sense them to have?
How big an area do they take up?
Is your focus of attention mainly outside or inside your body?
Are there other feelings, tastes or smells that seem important in the memory?

Experiment with the feelings as with the other submodalities. Make a note of the ones that are important.

Fill in a submodality worksheet with the results of your exercise. See overleaf for an example.

SUBMODALITY WORKSHEET – EXAMPLE

Event: **Tennis match, 17 August 1999**

Visual Submodalities	Memory	Comments
Associated/dissociated	associated	important
Distance	one foot away	important
Moving/still	moving	important
Speed	normal	
Location	straight ahead	important
Spread of visual field	full view with wide (peripheral) vision	
Colours /black and white		
	faint colours	
Colour intensity	very little	not important
Clarity	very clear	not important
Focus	good focus	
Size	large	no borders
Other	none	

NOTES

1   Narrowing the angle of vision made the memory much less intense.
2   Being associated was very important. When I was dissociated, the experience did not seem to be really mine
3   Distance was important. Moving the picture further away made it less intense. Moving it closer was uncomfortable.
4   Movement in the picture was important. Freeze frames took away the intensity of the memory.
5   The picture needed to be straight ahead. If I put it to one side or higher or lower, it was less comfortable.
6   Speed was important. Slower speed than normal was less intense, faster made it difficult to follow.

- associated
- distance – one foot away
- location – straight ahead
- full visual field with peripheral vision

Auditory Submodalities	Memory	Comments
Sounds/words	no words, sound of ball on racquet	good juicy sound
Direction	in front, from racquet	
Distance	one foot	
Rhythm	matching the play	
Location of sound	straight ahead	
Talking to self/silent	silent internally	important
Loudness	normal	
Length	normal	
Clarity	good	
Other	n/a	

NOTES
1 Sounds were not so important to the memory, but adding the sound of ball on racquet made it more satisfying.
2 Internal silence was very important.

CRITICAL SUBMODALITIES

- external sound only, no self-talk
- clear sound of ball hitting racquet

Kinesthetic Submodalities	Memory	Comments
Location	over my eyes, also in my hands	
Intensity	medium	
Temperature	comfortably warm	important
Shape	irregular	
Size	no boundaries, fading at the edges	important
Attention inside/outside	outside on the ball	very important
Other	fresh air, enjoyed the feeling of the air going into my lungs	

NOTES

1   A feeling of warmth is important (even though the court was cold at the time). Making the feeling cold made it unpleasant.
2   I was aware of bodily feeling, but an outside focus of attention was important.

CRITICAL SUBMODALITIES

- outside attention
- a warm feeling
- no clear boundaries to the feelings

SUMMARY

Critical Submodalities of Imagery for Mental Rehearsal

- picture one foot away, straight ahead, full visual field with peripheral vision, associated
- external sound, no self-talk, clear sound of ball hitting racquet
- outside attention, warm feelings, no clear boundaries on feelings

Effective Mental Rehearsal

There are some general guidelines I have found helpful for athletes working with imagery and critical submodalities:

■ *Pay attention to association and dissociation.*
Mental rehearsal must be associated, otherwise you will not be in the experience and you will not get the micro-muscle movements of the moves or critical information like your sense of balance. Dissociated mental imagery is useful in experimenting with different submodalities before stepping in and for learning after the game. *Mental rehearsal will only work well if you use associated imagery.*

■ *Use normal speed.*
When you rehearse mentally, you want to make it as 'lifelike' as possible. Imagine everything at the speed it would be in the game or event. If this is difficult, then start slowly and build up to normal speed – quick thinking leads to quick actions.

■ *Use your peripheral vision.*
We say a player is 'focused' when they are concentrated, but their vision will usually be 'wide open', taking in as wide an area as possible. When you use imagery, let your visual field be wide open and relaxed.

■ *Pay attention to what is happening outside, not inside.*
When you visualize, you will automatically pay attention to whatever is outside yourself – you do not see the inside of your eyelid! In the same way, pay attention to sounds from the outside, if there are any, and not your internal dialogue. Pay attention to the outward movements you are making, not to your internal bodily feelings.

The next exercise will give you the definitive way to improve with mental rehearsal.

Exercise 16: Using Imagery to Improve your Skills

Relax before you do this exercise. Imagery is more effective when your body is relaxed. Find a time when you will not be disturbed.

Decide which sports technique you want to improve with imagery.

Stage 1: Your Ideal Practice Place

Create an ideal place where you want to practise. Your real facilities may not be perfect, but your mental ones will be. Imagine a court, a field, a track, a green that is perfect in every way. Look around, listen to and touch your ideal place. Create it in as much detail as possible, make it a pleasure to be in. Add whatever equipment you want. You can even put in cheering spectators or a few close friends to encourage you.

Stage 2: See the Technique or Skill Dissociated

Imagine you are a spectator. See yourself from the outside playing absolutely perfectly. If this is difficult, then imagine a really good player and use them as a model. Watch and listen carefully (you are not associated, so you will not yet have the feelings that go with the imagery). Make sure you use all your critical submodalities for the picture and sounds. When you are absolutely sure that what you see is perfect in every detail, associate into the image.

Stage 3: Associated Mental Rehearsal

Now mentally rehearse the skill while you are associated. Check that your imagery has all your critical submodalities. Enjoy the feeling. You cannot go wrong! You are playing perfectly. You need never miss a goal kick, a putt or a serve when you use imagery. If for any reason you are not satisfied, dissociate and go back to Stage 2. Watch the image again until you are satisfied, then step in and associate again. It may help to look down as you do this to help access the feelings of the movements.

Stage 4: Repeat

Repeat the associated imagery at least five times. It may not be so easy at first, but everything will become more clear and more streamlined as you repeat it. The effort you put in at the beginning will pay off in a big way later.

You can vary this exercise to suit specific events. Instead of your ideal practice ground, imagine the actual match venue. Make it as real as possible. Then do your mental rehearsal in those surroundings. If you do not know what the surroundings will be like exactly, imagine something as close as possible.

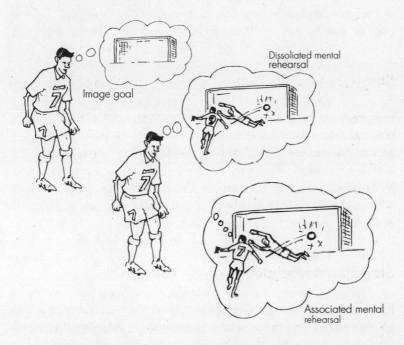

Figure 3.1: Performance enhancement with mental rehearsal.

The Principles of Imagery

1 *Start from your goal.* Your goal comes first. Imagine what it will be like to achieve it. See it in detail so you are absolutely clear about what you will have to do to achieve it.

2 *Focus on the process and not the result.* First set your goal and use your powers of imagery to be clear about what you want. Then use imagery to work on *how* you achieve it, not the goal itself. Control the process and provided you are clear about the goal, the result will flow naturally. Finally see the goal achieved as a result of the

process. For example, to mentally rehearse a putt, imagine selecting the right club, feel the weight of the club in your hand, settle yourself into position, go through your usual moves and focus on controlling the putt. Then watch the putt go into the hole. This is what separates imagery from daydreaming. Daydreaming focuses on the result; things happen by magic. Imagery focuses on the process and good results happen inevitably.

3 *Be specific.* Imagine as much detail as you can. The place you are in, the clothes you are wearing, every part of the skill you are rehearsing. The richer the detail, the more powerful the process.

4 *See, hear and feel perfection.* What you see is what you get. Don't be satisfied with second best; imagine everything exactly how you want it to be.

5 *Use all the senses.* The more senses you use, the more memorable the experience and the deeper its imprint. What is true on the outside is true for imagery. An intense experience engages all the senses. So, see the pictures in your imagination as clearly as you can. Hear the sounds, feel your body movements including your sense of balance. You can even imagine tastes and smells. You can taste the sweat on your lips and breathe in the fresh air.

6 *Relax.* Relaxation enhances the effects. Find a place where you can relax without distractions and concentrate completely on the imagery. When your body is relaxed, your mind is free. This is your chance to be an 'armchair athlete'. If anyone asks you what you are doing, you can reply with a straight face, 'I'm practising my sport!'

7 *Practise.* Perfect practice makes perfect execution. Also, the more you use imagery, the more skilled you will become at it and the better it will work for you. Make imagery part of your practice routine. Two or three ten-minute sessions a week work well.

What you have between your ears is a fantastic virtual reality machine. It costs nothing and it's always available, so use it well. You may not be able to physically train every day, but you can spend five minutes doing the mental rehearsal exercise above. Imagery is also useful in many other situations:

■ Use imagery if you cannot train because you are injured. Imagery will help you keep your skill even when you cannot play.

- Use it to prepare for a game or match. Imagine the conditions in as much detail as possible, especially if they will be difficult. Add driving rain to your mental rehearsal, or the roar of a home crowd cheering on the opposing team. You will be more prepared for the real thing if you have already rehearsed it mentally. Athletes from the Soviet Bloc were often not popular when they competed in international events at the height of the Cold War. Their coaches used to prepare them for this by training in a stadium with sounds of booing and insults being played over the loud-speaker system. The athletes probably did not like it, but when it happened for real, they were ready!
Imagery is the antidote to the psychological warfare that is becoming more and more prevalent in sport. For example, in cricket, close fielders like to welcome a new batsman with remarks like: 'Oh dear, the last batsman to face this bowler spent three weeks in traction...', 'Are your flies undone?', 'It's a long walk back to the pavilion...', 'I hear the local casualty department is very good...' You can take the sting out of this 'sledging' in any sport by imagining it first and preparing some snappy replies to deal with it.
- Use imagery to calm yourself at difficult stages in a match. We will deal with this in detail in Chapter 6.

New Perspectives

You need mental flexibility to change between different perspectives when you visualize – the associated perspective is quite different from the dissociated perspective, for example. There are other types of perspectives that you can use to improve your mental preparation and also your coaching skills.

The Performance Viewpoint

Think for a moment about what is important to you and what you like about your sport. Think, feel and remember – this is your experience. In NLP this is called *first position*. When you thought about your sport, that was where you were. First position is the 'performance spot'. There is just you and the challenge you face. Playing sport is a very first-position activity – you are right there in the heat of the game. You are in your own reality. There is nothing like physical exertion or pain to put you into first position.

The Coaching Viewpoint

When you make a leap of the imagination to experience what another person would think and feel, then you are in what NLP calls *second position*. We all have this skill – we can intuitively know how others feel, without being told, because we all share basic ways of feeling and reacting.

Second position is the coaching viewpoint. To be a good coach you need to know how your athletes feel and think so you can help in the way that suits them, not the way that suits you. Being able to take second position is the key to good coaching.

We often take second position without being completely aware that we are doing it. We have intuitions about how others feel. Second position is also the key to modelling and accelerated learning – we 'become' someone else to learn how they think and feel rather than getting them to tell us about it. We use second position when we are young to model adult skills. We also do it in a more informal way as adults. Have you ever watched an athlete on television and found yourself tensing your muscles in sympathy with them? I have seen friends throw themselves around the sofa during a football match and others clench and unclench their hands while watching a golf tournament. They are associated into second position, some part of their mind is 'with' the athlete.

The Referee Position

There is a third position, too, an ideal 'referee position'. Here you are watching yourself and taking an objective view of what happens. You may not like referees or umpires and the decisions they make, but they are meant to be impartial, they are part of the game, yet above it. This is also the position in which you can evaluate your own performance and learn from it.

First position is easy. You are there already. Try this exercise to test the strength of your second position.

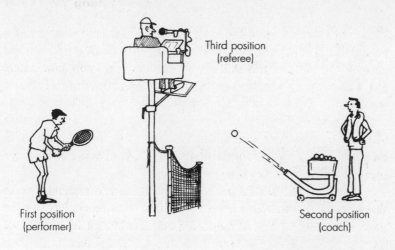

Figure 3.2: The three perspectives – performer, coach, referee

---

Exercise 17: A Record Leap of the Imagination

Think of someone you know well or someone you coach. Imagine what it would be like to be them for a few moments.

> How do they sit?
> What sort of things do they pay attention to?
> How do they speak?
> Imagine becoming that person.
> Now, as that person, what do you think of yourself, the athlete?
> How do you (as that person) feel about yourself (the athlete)?
> What kind of advice would you give yourself?

Now come back to yourself

This is a very useful exercise in three ways:

- First, as a coach, you need to understand your protégé, especially if you are having trouble building a good relationship with them.
- Secondly, the exercise will help you find out what your friends and family think of your sporting life. Sometimes it can take up more time than you think and they may be uncomfortable without actually telling you directly.
- Thirdly, you will be able to take second position with your opponent in a match. You will be able to get answers to questions like:
  What are they thinking?
  What do they think of you as an opponent?
  What kind of game plan do they have in mind?
  What do they see as your strengths and weaknesses?
  This is a really useful way to use second position. All great competitors are able to get inside the mind of their opponents and counter their plans. Your opponent will become your coach on how to beat them!
- Finally, the three positions can be used to enhance your imagery for match preparation.

Exercise 18: Performer, Coach, Referee

Imagine the place where you are going to play your next game or event. Imagine yourself there. If you have never been there, imagine what it might look like – your best guess.

Look around. What is it like? Claim your space. You belong here. You've earned it.

Imagine yourself there in first position as performer. Look around, see your opponent(s) and feel ready and confident, with a pleasant feeling of anticipation.

Enjoy that feeling for a moment.

Now shift to being a coach, one of your supporters, or one of your family or friends. Imagine you are one of them looking at you competing in the match.

What is it like being there?

What support can you give to yourself on the field?

Now change to being the third-position referee.

See yourself, the performer, getting ready to play.

What advice would you offer yourself?

What is important about this match?

Is there anything special you could to say about the venue, the match or your opponent?

Now come back to yourself. This is a general preparation for the match. The more important the match, the more you need to prepare.

Tennis player John Newcombe used a variation of this technique in his mental preparation. The night before, when the court was empty, he would go to the top of the stands, look down, open his arms and mentally embrace the whole scene. He imagined it was a close friend. It made him comfortable and at home in the place where he was competing the next day.

Imagery works. Jack Nicklaus has 100 victories in professional golf championships around the world. He has been awarded the title 'Golfer of the Century' twice and the 'PGA Player of the Year' award five times. He has earned over $8 million from the game. He is a fantastically good golfer. What is his mental strategy? He sees the result in his mind before he hits the ball. He says it's just like a movie. He never hits a shot, not even when practising, without a nice sharp focused mental film of what he wants to happen. First, he sees the ball where he wants it to land. He sees it clearly and in colour. Then he sees how the ball gets there. Then he sees himself making the swing that will make the ball do what he wants it to do. What an interesting description. Jack Nicklaus starts with the *goal*. Only when he knows what he wants does he imagine what he has to do to make it so. It sounds from his description as though he creates a dissociated picture and then steps into it. You may be thinking, 'If only I had those imagery skills! My mental movies are like home videos shot by someone who doesn't know one end of a video camera from the other.' But Jack Nicklaus says he does that for every shot he plays. So he practises imagery whenever he plays. No wonder he is good at it. Being a master of imagery must have contributed to his success. It can contribute to yours.

REFERENCES

Kolonay, B. J., 'The effects of visio-motor behaviour rehearsal on athletic performance', Masters thesis, Hunter College, City University of New York, 1977

Lane, J., 'Improving athletic performance through visio-motor behaviour rehearsal' in R. Suinn (ed.), *Psychology in Sports Methods and Applications*, Burgess, 1980

Nicklaus, Jack, *Golf my Way*, Simon and Schuster, 1974

Suinn, R., 'Imagery' in R. N. Singer, M. Murphey and L. Tennant (eds), *Handbook of Research on Sports Psychology*, Macmillan, 1993

CHAPTER THREE SUMMARY

We use our senses to experience the outside world and we think in remembered and constructed pictures, sounds, feelings, tastes and smells.

>When we think, we re-experience or re-present the world to ourselves through our inner senses, called *representational systems* in NLP.

>We use our representational systems for sports imagery and mental rehearsal.

>Imagery uses the power of your imagination. Once you have set your goals, imagery programmes your body and mind to achieve them.

>Imagery is used for:

■ improving a technical skill
■ counteracting negative images of mistakes
■ pre-match relaxation
■ gaining energy and confidence before a game
■ working out tactics before the game
■ general preparation when you do not know exactly what to expect
■ calming yourself if you are tense during a match
■ learning from your game
■ healing sports injuries

>Imagery works by:

■ Programming your muscles to react in the way you want. Thinking of an action induces micro-muscle movements that mimic what happens when you really perform that action.
■ Providing a blueprint for success.
■ Giving you confidence by making the actions familiar.

>Imagery involves using all the senses.

>>The clearer and more controllable your mental images, the more effective your mental rehearsal will be.

We all have a preferred way of thinking — certain representational systems are easier to use than others.

You can find out your preferred way of thinking by analysing
the *predicates* (sensory-specific words) you use.

All the senses have qualities — pictures have size, shape and
distance, for example. These qualities are called *submodalities*.

One important submodality distinction is between association and dissociation.

- *Association* is when you imagine seeing out of your own eyes,
you are in your body. Mental rehearsal must be associated
otherwise it will not be effective. Only when you imagine you are
in your body will your muscles respond to your images.
- *Dissociation* means you are seeing yourself in the picture; you
imagine you are outside your body. Dissociation is good for
learning and setting up perfect mental rehearsal.

Some submodalities will be critical to get the most out of
mental rehearsal.

The best sequence for mental rehearsal is:

1 Imagine your ideal practice place.
2 See the technique or skill dissociated.
3 Mentally rehearse with associated imagery.

There are the seven principles for successful imagery:

1 Set the goal.
2 Focus on the process and not the result.
3 Be specific.
4 See perfection.
5 Use all the senses.
6 Relax.
7 Practise.

Imagery uses different perspectives. There are three main perspectives in NLP:

1 *First position.* Your own reality – 'the performer's viewpoint'.
2 *Second position.* Another person's reality – 'the coach's viewpoint'.
3 *Third position.* The outside evaluation position – 'the referee's viewpoint'.

- First position is where you are when your play your sport.
- Second position is useful for coaching and understanding your opponent's tactics.
- Third position is useful for evaluating your performance objectively.

In the Zone

The Zone and the Pits

You've set your goals and you're committed to them. You've trained hard and used imagery to thoroughly prepare yourself. Now you walk out onto the field, the court or the track. It's time. You deserve to do well; you have done everything you can. Now you have to concentrate and keep your mind still as it tries to skip about like a cat on hot coals and is as hard to bring to the point as a politician. Once the game begins the quality of your concentration is a deciding factor. Your performance varies as your concentration varies.

The quality of concentration has two extremes and you have probably visited both of them. On one hand there are 'the pits'. Nothing goes right. You miss easy chances; your mind wanders, it gets lost and loses its map, its compass and its mobile phone. You go through the motions, but somehow your game never flows. You find you are distracted by all sorts of trivia. You may feel resigned or angry, but win or lose, you know you can do better.

The other extreme is 'the zone'. Here you just know that everything you do will be right. You play and everything flows. You don't have to try, there's no effort. It's like stepping into the sun from a room lit by artificial light. If only it could be like this every time. Even if you don't win, the match goes down in your personal history. In the zone you are focused, your mind is as clear as a crystal pool; there is no sense of strain, no furrowed brow and no hunched shoulders. You can't *try* to get into the zone. It comes and goes and leaves no footprints.

You will probably experience the zone with roughly the same frequency as you experience the pits. Most of the time you will be between the two, though hopefully nearer the zone than the pits. What can you do to visit the zone more often and leave the pits a distant memory?

Concentration

The zone is where your quality of concentration is at its highest. What is concentration? Think about it for a moment. We say concentration can be 'increased', 'decreased', 'lost' or 'broken'. What does it bring to your mind? Many people get a still picture of themselves staring at something. Now think of 'concentrating'. What sort of image does that bring to mind? This usually creates a moving picture. Concentration is not a thing, it's a process, something we do. Concentration also means making a solution stronger by putting more resources in. What is the solution? Attention is the solution. When we concentrate, we give attention. Rather than think about 'concentration' in the abstract we have to ask some different questions: how do you pay attention, and to what?

Attention has two sides – paying attention to some parts of your experience means deleting other parts from your awareness. This ability to delete is very important. My daughter can do her homework while listening to music, for example, while I can't work with music on – it's too distracting because my thinking relies more on internal sounds than hers does. Everyone deletes some things automatically. We have to – we are bombarded with possible sights, sounds and feelings every second of the day. Look at the colours around you – colours that you were not aware of until now. Listen to the sounds all around that you did not hear until a moment ago. What feelings do you have now? How is your left elbow? What smells are in the room? What tastes in your mouth? These are all things that might have grabbed your attention but did not. You did not make an effort to keep them out. As soon as you concentrated on reading this book, they dropped out of your attention naturally. In fact the only way you could have made them into a continuing distraction would have been to think, 'I mustn't think of my left elbow. . .' That way you would have to continue thinking of your left elbow in order to know what not to think of.

We pay attention to difference. When something changes, we notice. If your elbow started to hurt, you would notice it. If there were a smell of smoke in the room, you would certainly notice it and fast. Things that are initially distracting (like loud background music), on the other hand, eventually cease to be a distraction when you get used to them.

So, we know how to pay attention, how to concentrate in everyday life. We need to transfer that ability to the match.

There are three principles of concentration:

1   Concentration is natural and easy. Everyone does it. You are doing it now. We concentrate by selectively paying attention to what is important to us and blotting out the rest.
2   We pay attention to significant change, so we can control distractions by what we define as significant.
3   When we focus on what is important to us, distractions disappear automatically. The more we try to get rid of distractions, the more troublesome they are likely to be, because the more attention we are giving them.

The Light of Attention

Concentration is often called 'focus'. This is a nice metaphor because it makes you think of the mind like a searchlight. Attention is the light source. You turn it where you choose. Whatever you look at, there will be areas of darkness around, but you would see what was there if you changed the angle of the light. Normally the light is quite diffuse. Concentration is the lens you put in the searchlight to focus the light in the way you want.

Figure 4.1: The searchlight of attention

The first important question is *how* you pay attention. The light of attention can have a narrow or a broad focus. For a narrow focus, look closely at this book. Pick out the details. Notice the colour of the page, the blackness of the print. See the small imperfections in the letters. You have narrowed your attention and you have also narrowed your visual field. To pick out the letters you have to take your attention from your surroundings. The more detail you pick out, the less you see. The same principle applies to sound and feelings. You can narrow your focus of attention and analyse a sound or a feeling in detail.

Now, for a broad focus, let your attention go wide. Look out around the room. See as much as possible, without picking out the details. You have changed the lens in the light to one that shines less light over more objects.

The second question is *what* you pay attention to. Where do you direct the light? Again there are two main possibilities – internal and external. When you narrowed and broadened your focus of attention a few minutes ago, you looked externally. Now do the same thing internally. Narrow your focus of attention to one small part of your body. Experience the nuances of feeling there.

Now change the lens. Broaden your focus of attention so that you have full body awareness. Be aware of the feelings of your whole body.

Internal and external attention are not exclusive; we constantly move between the two throughout the day. Most of the time, we direct our attention broadly outward, otherwise we would walk into people or trip over. Pain and discomfort will usually draw your attention internally on a narrow focus. These distinctions of broad and narrow, internal and external, originally proposed by the sports psychologist Nideffer in 1976, are very useful in analysing your game.

Figure 4.2: Direction outwards, direction inwards

When you think of concentrating in the match, think where and how
you need to direct your attention. You have four possibilities, depending on what you want to do. Throughout the game, your attention will
shift between these four styles as shown in Figure 4.2.

The top left-hand corner is narrow attention focused outwards.
This is the 'watch the ball' corner. You need this kind of attention when
you catch a ball in cricket. Golfers need it to focus on the lie of the ball
for a putt on the green. Tennis players need it to follow a swirling lob.

The top right part is where your attention goes out on a broad
focus – the 'follow the game' corner. A footballer will pay attention in
this way as they manoeuvre for position, a tennis player when they
survey the court, a runner when they track the position of the field, a
batsman when they survey the field before taking guard.

The bottom left quadrant is the narrow focus inward. This is the
imagery corner. When you go inside yourself and mentally rehearse, or
calm yourself with soothing imagery, this is where your attention will
be drawn. On the negative side, this is where your attention will be
taken if you are injured. The pain will pull your attention in like a
magnet pulls a compass. You may also be pulled here by self-talk. This

corner is not a good place to be when you are in the midst of a game. It will take the attention from where it is needed – on the game.

The bottom right quadrant is the broad internal focus. This is the energy balance corner where you check your own feelings, your emotional state, your energy reserves, your confidence, anxiety and enjoyment. This is also the kind of attention you need to work out tactics and strategy during a game, to decide what plays to make or what your next move will be.

Your attention will flicker into all of these areas when you are playing, although during a game you want your attention to be mostly external – you want to be experiencing the outside world. This is called *uptime* in NLP. Your attention is turned outward; your body is responding. You are certainly thinking and planning, but that is in the background, it does not draw your attention. In all games, though, there are also times when you need to look internally, to review and decide tactics before turning your attention outwards again. This is called *downtime* in NLP. Imagery practice, mental preparation, the post-game review and planning strategy are all handled best in downtime.

Given that your attention is always somewhere among the quadrants, what are distractions?

Distractions are when your focus of attention is not in the right place at the right time.

For example, you may need to plan strategy with a broad internal focus, but your opponent distracts you and demands your narrow outward attention. However, most distractions come from an internal narrow focus on thoughts and feelings when you need to be paying broad external attention to the game.

These four styles of attention not only describe how your attention fluctuates during a game, but also broad styles of play, like preferred ways of thinking. You may recognize that you have a tendency towards one type of attention. If you favour a broad internal style then you will play more by 'gut feeling'. You think out the game beforehand and pay attention to your feelings. You concentrate on your own game rather than on your opponent. The danger with this style is that you may overanalyse a game, even when it is in progress, and lose your focus in the present moment.

A narrow internal style makes you very good at critical self-analysis, especially after a match. You are excellent at finding errors and analysing tactics. The danger here is that you become too self-critical and lose confidence. Mistakes may be hard to forget, making it difficult to concentrate externally. You will tend to set more store by what goes wrong than what goes right and self-talk may distract you when you need to focus outward.

The third style is that of broad external attention. This style gives you great spatial awareness and tactical information, and you can keep track of other people on the field very easily. The danger is that you overload yourself and do not discriminate between important information and what can be safely ignored. You may also miss quick opportunities that need a narrow focus of attention.

Finally, the narrow external style keeps a hawk-like eye on the ball. This is very useful for sports like golf and bowls, which need attention to detail at critical points. The danger of this style is becoming too narrowly focused and losing the wider picture. You may watch the ball and hit it well, but fail to notice that your opponent is perfectly placed to intercept it. You will not be strong where tactics are fluid and the game is changing rapidly. This style of attention is more suited to golf than team sports.

These styles of attention seem to correlate with extroversion and introversion. Extroverts pay more attention to what is happening on the outside, introverts to their own internal world. Different styles suit different sports and the sport you enjoy and improve in will be the one that suits your style. Stress may catapult us into our preferred style, often with disastrous results; this is usually how lapses of concentration occur.

No style is better; the balance is important. Don't get stuck in one style. You need a narrow internal focus when doing your imagery and a broad internal focus when working with outcomes and planning your strategy. During the match you need broad external focus to appraise the situation, switching to an internal focus to change tactics or analyse the game. You also need an internal focus during the game to manage your own emotional state and monitor your energy. You may also need a narrow internal focus at critical points to 'watch the ball'.

Visual and kinesthetic attention is critical in nearly all sports – you need to see what is happening and have a strong sense of balance and body awareness. The auditory side is usually neglected. We all know the exhortation '*Watch* the ball!' but sometimes this may not help. You may be watching the ball and still not striking it very well. You can get stuck in a rut where the more you watch the ball, the more you mishit it. Shifting your attention to the sound of the ball can be very helpful sometimes. When you strike a golf or tennis ball in the right way you are rewarded with a satisfying sound. You know before you see the ball fly off whether you have really timed it by the sound it makes.

If your sport involves hitting or kicking a ball, experiment with the auditory sense. Try to get that juicy sound of a well-timed shot. I have used this technique with squash players. Rather than exhorting them to watch the ball, hit it hard and time it right, I ask them to listen to the sound as it hits their racquet. Soon they know exactly what sound they want – a satisfying 'clunk' of rubber on nylon strings. Then instead of asking them directly to try to time it, I ask them to hit the ball so that they produce that exact sound. When they get the sound, they automatically get a powerful and precise stroke. The end result is the same, but their attention is in a different place. Other times I will direct their attention to their feelings of balance, because when they are perfectly balanced, they hit the ball more cleanly. One of the most important secrets of successful coaching is to know where to direct the player's attention.

What sort of concentration style do you favour? Where are your strengths? Where are your weaknesses?

The practical way to apply these styles of concentration is to analyse the critical moments in your sport and see what kind of attention they need.

Exercise 19: Critical Concentration Points

1 *Relax and review your game.* Imagine how a typical game unfolds. What are the critical points where you need to pay close attention? These will be points where a mistake will cost you dear. For example, in tennis, serving or receiving a serve are critical, in golf it is preparing for a shot. Tackling or evading a tackle are critical in football. In cricket the batsman preparing to receive the next ball must be totally focused, as must be the bowler running in to bowl. Some sports, like golf, demand a high focus for a short time, others, like football, need a broader concentration that is more evenly spread throughout the game.

Find three or four key points in your game where you absolutely *have* to concentrate.

2 *Look at these critical points.* Which of the four types of concentration do you need to bring to them?

Do you need a narrow laser-like concentration focused outward on one or two key people?

Does your sport have any critical 'watch the ball' points?

Do you need a broad focus of attention outwards to know what is going on around you?

Or do you need to be focused internally at the critical point?

Some critical points will need two types of concentration in succession. For example, when you prepare a tennis serve, you first need a broad internal attention to decide where to place the ball and to gather your resources for the point. Then you need a narrow external focus on the ball as you lift it up, watch it carefully and hit it powerfully towards your opponent.

3 *Are there any times when you typically lose concentration?*

It may be in one of these critical areas, but need not be.

What happens to the quality of your concentration at these points? Where should it be and which of the other four styles does it jump to?

This exercise will give you the critical points in your sport and identify any other points when your attention is not where it should be.

How to Concentrate

How can you keep your concentration at these vital moments? You need an automatic process, one that does not need your attention at the time, because if you have to *think* about concentrating, then you are not concentrating! You want a way to automatically shift your attention to where it needs to go. You need to be unconsciously competent, nothing else will do.

The four concentration styles are states of mind – a combination of our thoughts, feelings, emotions, physical and mental energy. The power to concentrate is the ability to shift your state at will, so it is worth looking at how we usually shift from state to state during the day. It is not usually by choice. Our state of mind fluctuates continuously, mostly under the influence of outside events. We rarely think about choosing our emotional states, we are used to simply accepting them as they arise. Sometimes we go through the day just reacting to what happens. Then we go into a game expecting to be able to concentrate to order!

How do we change from state to state? By seeing, hearing or feeling something different and responding to it. The associations we make to these experiences automatically trigger our states. Most of the time we do not notice these triggers because they are so familiar and habitual. Think of the people and things that affect your state of mind during the day. Somebody walks into the office and you feel down because you know they usually have bad news. You see a friend and feel good because you have had many good experiences with them in the past. When you look out of the window at the rain and threatening sky with clouds that seem to be only a few feet off the pavement, you might feel a little depressed. The next day the sun is shining and you feel happier. You hear some of your favourite music and feel happy. When the signature tune for a well-known programme strikes up on the radio you might switch off immediately (I do). Music powerfully affects our moods. So, we anticipate good or bad feelings based on our past experience, and our brain doesn't wait, it sees, hears or feels the trigger, makes the association and jumps into the feeling straightaway. The state of mind gets linked to the trigger because it happens regularly and consistently. We practise it (although not deliberately) and that builds unconscious competence in responding to the trigger. These triggers do not even need good or bad feelings associated with them. They may be neutral. You stop at a red light without thinking because red lights mean stop.

These triggers work because they happen all the time and so they become habitual. Everyday life consists of a series of habits and they are very useful, we do not want to have to think about what a red light means every time we approach it.

We can apply our facility to respond to these triggers in sport, only we need to build the associations consciously rather than letting them happen at random. Physical habits may take time to build, but the brain learns faster than the body, so you can establish mental habits very quickly.

You want to set up triggers that will reliably and automatically take you into the state of concentration you want. NLP calls these triggers *anchors*, and the process of setting up the triggers and rituals is called *anchoring*. The way to set up a trigger is to establish a small ritual that you do consistently. You'll see top athletes do this on television. For example, watch tennis players as they prepare to serve – a critical moment in the game. The basics of serving are simple. You throw the ball up and hit it. Watch carefully what they actually do. They take the ball, look at it, bounce it two or three times, look up, shuffle their feet and then wind themselves up into the serve like coiling a spring. These preliminary movements are all part of the total action – serving. Their purpose is to streamline the action and achieve the focus they need to propel the ball towards their opponent at speeds approaching 120 miles per hour. Watch the player getting ready to receive the serve and you will see similar rituals as they get the state of concentration they need to react fast. Watch batsmen in Test cricket get ready to receive a ball, or the bowler at the end of their run up preparing to bowl. The rituals athletes perform at these critical times put them in a tunnel of concentration and help to block out distractions. Golfers usually have a meticulous pre-shot routine. If they are interrupted, they will usually stop and start the routine all over again from the beginning.

These rituals work for the world-class players and they will work for every standard of play. NLP models what works. You don't need to model exactly *what* these athletes do; you model the *process* they use to get in the right state. The process associates useful states of concentration with specific behavioural triggers or anchors.

Exercise 20: Making your Ritual

1 Take the first critical point you identified from the last exercise. What quality of concentration do you need?

2 Now think of a time when you had that quality of concentration. Sometime in your life, you have had that state of mind that you need now, perhaps in another part of your game or maybe in a completely different situation. That state is a resource from the past that you will bring to the present with an anchor.

3 When you have identified such a time, imagine yourself back then, associate into the memory and experience it again as fully as you can.

4 Next you need a trigger for that state.

While you are in that state of concentration:

■ Pick a word or phrase that links strongly with that state of concentration, for example 'focus' or 'laser' or 'still'.

■ Pick a visual trigger, something that you know you will be able to see in that situation, your racquet perhaps, or the ball or your hand. Make this trigger very specific, for example not just the ball but the intricate patterning on the ball, the criss-cross of the strings of your racquet or the pattern of veins on the back of your hand. It does not matter what it is, only that you link it with the state.

■ Now pick a kinesthetic or feeling trigger. Taking a deep breath is a good example, or breathing out purposefully. You could wipe your hand on your shirt or leg. The trigger should be a natural movement that you can do easily; the only attention you want to attract is your own, not that of curious spectators wondering what you are doing!

■ Now test the trigger that you have set up. Say the phrase to yourself, see the visual cue or, if that is impossible, imagine it in your mind, and make the gesture. Notice how that changes your state of concentration.

■ If the trigger does not work, go back to Step 4. Associate as fully as you can into that state, be fully back in that time, hearing what you heard, seeing what you saw, feeling what you felt. Then set your triggers again

The triggers will catch the state you are in when you set them. Use all three to begin with, but later you may find one is enough. The reason for setting three is that uses all the representational systems. The best trigger to use is the one in your preferred representational system. These triggers make up your ritual.

5 Mentally rehearse using the triggers. Imagine yourself at a critical concentration point in a game. Imagine using the triggers. Mentally rehearse what you want to happen. Make sure you are associated, as if you were there, seeing out of your own eyes. The point of this is to make sure you remember to use the triggers in a game.

6 Practise these triggers consistently. Having a great ritual that will reliably get you into a focused state is the first step; the second step is to remember to use it. The more you practise, the more the triggers will pass into unconscious competence so you will do them automatically and they will work automatically.

EXAMPLES OF ANCHORS FOR CONCENTRATION

Critical Point	Concentration Required	Anchor
Taking a free kick	Focus: Narrow Direction: Outwards	Sound: 'Fire!' Visual: Pattern on the ball Feeling: Deep breath
Kick off	Focus: Broad Direction: Outwards	Sound: 'Go!' Visual: Opposing team member Feeling: Make fist

There are three main reasons why this ritual may not work immediately:

1 The state of concentration you achieved in Step 4 may not have been strong enough. Make sure you have a strong, robust state.
2 You haven't practised it enough. At least 20 repetitions are needed to learn these sorts of skills and they need to be fairly close together, otherwise the effect fades.
3 You may try to use the triggers when you are already in a strong negative emotional state. This will overpower the state you are trying to achieve. For example if you are angry and upset during the game, these triggers may not be enough to calm you and put you into a focused state.

Trying to use anchors when you are upset is known as the 'reverse anchor trap'. This is how it works. A player gets angry or upset and loses concentration. They try to use their concentration ritual, but they are too angry and that energy works against the concentration they are trying to achieve. They are like a driver trying to put the car into first gear when they are already going backwards in reverse. The result is a nasty grating sound as the gears crash and the car stalls. If the player consistently crashes their gears like this, trying to counteract a strong angry state, *the concentration anchor becomes associated with the angry state – the exact opposite of what they want!* Once this happens then the triggers will not take the player to a state of concentration, but of anger. So they may conclude that mental training doesn't work. Unfortunately it is working all too well, but in the opposite direction! What's the answer? The player needs a 'neutral' anchor, a way to break the bad state they are in so their anchor will move them to the focused state they want.

Exercise 21: Setting a Neutral Anchor

1 Check you feel in a neutral state right now.
2 Pick a word or phrase to associate with this state. Jokes are excellent as break states. I know a football player who asked his teammates to tell him a joke whenever he got upset. Set up a joke, funny story or funny incident you can remember to change your state. Pick a visual scene, perhaps one that goes with the joke or funny incident. Pick an action, maybe pinching yourself or taking a deep breath (but make it different from the concentration anchor!)
3 Mentally rehearse using the anchor. Imagine some incident in your game when you tend to get angry or upset – a bad line call, a mishit shot or a bad tackle by an opposing team member. You may feel a little angry just thinking about it. Now imagine using your neutral anchor and notice how it takes you out of that state.

You will still need to practise this anchor to test it – and of course remember to use it. Many athletes have some great anchors that work well, but in the heat of the moment they forget to use them, so they might as well not have them. Part of the benefit of mental rehearsal is to help you remember to use your skills when you need them. The more you use them, the better they will work. Then you will have a choice – to stay angry, upset and ineffectual, or to 'break state' and then reclaim your focus.

The more skills you can bring to unconscious competence, the more you can concentrate on building other skills you need. Think about the performance routines you can establish. The American sports psychologist Jim Loehr developed a '16-second routine' for tennis players. They learned to do it between *every* point, regardless of the state of the match, to keep their concentration. First they transferred the racquet to their non-playing hand, then relaxed their playing arm, paced up and

down a few times and did some positive imagery. This sort of performance routine is a good idea, because if you get into the habit of doing
it every time, you are more likely to remember it when you really need
it. It is not a failure to 'lose' concentration, but if you do, these anchors
will help you to 'find' it again.

Concentration has two great enemies, one mental and one physical
– anxiety and fatigue. Anxiety will be dealt with in the next chapter.
As for fatigue, that is physical – we can put mind over matter only for
so long, then the matter fights back.

Whatever the cause, a lapse of concentration can undo all the
previous efforts. This is true particularly in tennis. Sometimes what
separates the winner from the loser is a wafer-thin difference in
concentration at a crucial point. I remember an exciting Davis Cup
match between Greg Rusedski and Jim Courier at Birmingham in 1999.
There seemed to be a bit of a personal edge in the match and it was
also crucial in the overall result. Courier won the first set six–four.
Rusedski took the second on a tiebreak. Courier won the third six
games to three. Rusedski came back and won the next set by six games
to one. This could have broken Courier's concentration, but the deciding set was immensely exciting. It reached four games all. Both players
held their serve until Courier was six games to five ahead. Now
Rusedski needed all his concentration to hold his serve or all his efforts
over the last three hours would be for nothing. The game reached 30
all, then Rusedski produced two aces to level the score six games all.
Courier took his service game and Rusedski then served two double
faults and was suddenly love–30 down. A couple of weak returns from
Rusedski gave Courier the match in 3 hours, 47 minutes. Both men
must have been desperately tired, but the defining moment was those
last four points. Courier was able to keep his focus when he needed to.

The Zone

When the swordsman stands against his opponent, he is not to think of
the opponent, nor of himself, nor of his enemy's sword movements. He
just stands there with his sword, which, forgetful of all technique, is ready
only to allow the dictates of the unconscious. The man has effaced himself as the wielder of the sword. When he strikes, it is not the man but the
sword in the hand of the unconscious that strikes.

Takuan

Concentration is your entry ticket to the zone, the place we all want to go. The zone is also known as 'the flow state' because there everything flows easily and naturally. Everything seems effortless. For a runner the race is easy. For a footballer the ball seems to be attracted to their boots like metal to magnets. For a golfer, the hole pulls the ball in like a whirlpool sucks a paper boat. For a tennis player the ball seems like a fluffy football, floating like a puffball on the breeze. And afterwards, these athletes 'wake up', join the mundane world and feel they have played a special game. They will be tired, but perhaps not as tired as usual. The game seems to have played itself, in the spirit of the opening quotation from the master Japanese swordsman Takuan.

The zone has a paradox at its heart. The moment you realize you are there and start congratulating yourself, you have popped out of it. You can't be there and analyse it at the same time. To think about it, you have to be outside it. It is like a living creature, it dies when you try to dissect it.

You can only play at your best and enter the zone by letting go of your conscious preparation and let unconscious competence take you towards mastery. Your physical and mental practice is over, your conscious analysis is complete and you have to let go and trust your unconscious. Then you are in a state of 'no mind'. You act without conscious effort and what you do has a flowing quality, like hitting through the ball in golf as opposed to trying to steer it. The relationship of your conscious mind to your unconscious is like that of a rider and a horse. The rider tells the horse the direction in which to go, but the horse supplies the power. The rider is the guide, but must not tell the horse where to put its feet.

You will always know when you have been in the zone. It has three unmistakable qualities, the same qualities you need to play at your best:

1 No trying – the play is effortless, you do not have to try.
2 No thinking – you are unselfconscious, you do not have to think about what to do.
3 No past or future – you are in the present moment, all that matters is what is happening now.

Unconscious Process

A very interesting piece of research was published in 1999. Dr David Collins, a sports psychologist from the University of Surrey, monitored the brains of athletes and found that electrical activity was at a minimum before success. He used four electrodes to measure brain activity before karate martial artists attempted to break a three-inch plank of wood, before football players took a penalty and before cricketers tried to throw in and hit the wicket. A certain low electrical brain activity called alpha waves peaked before the athletes were successful. Alpha meant 'ready'. Dr Collins then tested the findings with archers by getting them to shoot only when the alpha activity peaked and he found they shot more accurately.

David Collins' research was concerned with sports where the athletes had time to prepare themselves. There are many sports where this is not possible, where you have to make split-second decisions. Another piece of interesting research, by Dr Robert Adair of Yale University, was presented to the Conference of the American Association of Science in New York in February 2000. Dr Adair analysed reaction times for striking a baseball. A baseball striker has about 400 milliseconds – about the time it takes to blink three times – to analyse the ball coming towards them, swing the bat and hit the ball. A baseball swing takes 150 milliseconds, so it must start 250 milliseconds after the ball is released. Of course the ball has got to travel some distance before the eye and brain have enough information about its trajectory to make a decision on how to hit it. That takes about 175 milliseconds. So the window of opportunity to register the ball and decide what to do is just 75 milliseconds. It takes 45 milliseconds for the eye and brain to register the ball as it approaches from the pitcher's hand. When we do the maths that leaves 30 milliseconds to decide the stroke – that is less than the time it takes to blink. Can the batsman decide consciously? Never. It's done by unconscious process. The same sort of blink-of-an-eye decisions take place in cricket when a fast bowler hurls a hard leather ball at the batsman at speeds approaching 100 miles an hour and in tennis in the professional men's game when players are facing a serve.

The conscious mind is too slow to cope with the speed of such decisions. In the zone you are outside conscious control. Like a rider on a galloping horse, there is exhilarating power and speed, but hardly any control of exactly what the horse does. Both must trust each other.

In the zone it is your conscious and unconscious that work together. To enter the zone, the first step is to build trust between conscious and unconscious.

The unconscious gets a bad press sometimes as a Freudian hotbed of anti-social criminal desires that are just about kept in check by a veneer of civilization, like a prison for the criminally insane where the inmates are always trying to escape. However this is not the whole truth. The unconscious contains all your potential, everything you are not aware of right now. It has heights as well as depths and most of it is involved in the mundane task of keeping you alive. You do not consciously manage your physical body; your unconscious does. You breathe, your heart beats, your digestive system works without your conscious mind having to make it all happen. These processes work best when you do not interfere. You cannot deliberately and directly make your heart beat faster or slower, unless you have had training in yoga. What you can do is think of someone you love and that will make your heart beat faster. You cannot make your digestion work any quicker or slower directly, but you can eat different types of food to influence how it works. We have influence but not control over these unconscious processes. When they work well, you are healthy. What we want to do is to harness the power of unconscious process in order to play sport better. (Although I am writing about 'the unconscious' here, this is shorthand for all the processes that take place outside your conscious awareness. It is part of living.)

Have you ever got into your car and driven off, only to 'wake up' a few minutes later realizing that you have driven some miles without really paying conscious attention to either your driving or where you were going? Driving is not easy, but you were safe, you drove the car and navigated the roads safely, even though you were not consciously aware but were in a kind of trance, a state of 'downtime'. If there had been a dangerous situation, then you would have got a wake up call from your unconscious: 'Hey! I need some guidance here!' At any time probably half the cars on the road are being driven by unconscious process and they don't usually hit each other. You can trust the unconscious process with your life. You trust it to keep your heart beating as well as to drive your car, so you can certainly trust it to help you improve at your sport!

This won't happen automatically, however. To improve in sport, you need to get a little better acquainted with your unconscious.

Unconscious process does not use language. It cannot shout in your ear to make you slow down, speed up or stop what you are doing. It communicates by feelings and intuitions, so you need to pay attention to these.

Get in harmony with your unconscious by:

■ *Treating your body well and taking care of yourself.* Taking care of yourself mean getting adequate and good-quality sleep, exercising enough but not too much and eating well and regularly.
■ *Listening and paying attention to your feelings and intuitions about what to do.* To become more intuitive means listening to the subtle signals your body gives you, particularly when you feel uneasy for no apparent reason.

Congruence

When conscious and unconscious are in agreement, you are *congruent*. All the different aspects of you are saying 'Yes!' and there is no need to hold back. The whole team knows what to do. When you are congruent members of your internal team are all playing the same game and following the same strategy.

The opposite is being *incongruent*. Something is out of tune, the picture is not complete, you feel something is wrong but do not know exactly what. Incongruence shows that you have noticed something that tells you something is not quite right, something needs further thought and preparation. The specific information you need has not yet broken the surface of consciousness, but it is there. This is the equivalent of a disorganized team: they don't quite know what they are doing, at least one team member is not clear about their role. Suppose you were in a football team where the players didn't get on and couldn't agree a strategy. Would you back them to win against another team that played well together? I wouldn't. Or suppose 10 are good but the goalkeeper is poor – a team is as good as its weakest link. So, when you play your game, you want to make sure your internal team is fully together, all committed. There is nothing wrong with being incongruent, however. It is very useful to know if a team member is weak. Then you can cover for them and then give them the training they need.

The next exercise is one to test your inner team, so that you can judge how congruent you are in any situation. It will also help you build your intuition and get more in touch with your unconscious processes, because it involves listening to the subtle signals you often ignore.

Exercise 22: The Inner Team

Relax and think back to a time when you were really committed and had no doubts about what to do. You were really congruent. It could be any time in your life, not necessarily to do with sport. Remember that time vividly, go back and associate into that experience as if it were happening now. Relive the event. Be aware of your feelings and imagery:

What is it like to feel congruent?
How does your body feel?
What sort of words and phrases are you saying to yourself?
What sort of tone of voice are you using?
What is the quality of the imagery you experience?

Pick something that you can use as a signal that seems to define the experience. It will usually be a feeling, perhaps in a particular part of your body, but it may be a tone of voice that you are using, or a particular picture quality. When you have the signal for the first experience, pick two more experiences of congruence when you felt the same way. Make one of them a sporting example if possible.

List the feeling, imagery and critical submodalities of each.

Which signal do these three experiences have in common?

Next, try to reproduce that exact same signal, but without going back into any of the experiences. Try to *consciously* create the same experience. If you can, then the signal you have chosen will not work, because it is not a genuine unconscious signal. When you find a signal that you cannot reproduce without associating back into the original experience then this is your *congruence signal*. It is the sound of your inner team all saying, 'Yes!'

Congruence is not a quality you either have or have not. Some times you will be more congruent, some times less so, just as a team will play better on some occasions than on others. The choice is not between a fantastic display of teamwork and utter disaster. So the best kind of signal to have is one where you can feel the *degree* of congruence – the stronger the signal, the more congruent you feel. For example, the signal you find might be a particular feeling in your stomach. The more you feel it, the more congruent you are. Or it might be a special internal voice tone – the louder you hear it, the more congruent you will be.

You can find your *incongruence signal* in a similar way. This is the signal which shows you that the inner team should not be allowed on the field until you find out what is wrong. To find your incongruence signal, pick three instances where you had serious reservations about some course of action. Perhaps you did not know why at the time, it just did not seem right to you. A good place to look for incongruence signals is when you invest or lend money. Alternatively, think of three projects you would never consider and explore your internal sights, sounds and feelings about those. Find the signal that is the same in all three instances and that you cannot fake or consciously reproduce. This is your incongruence signal; it is your intuition telling you not to proceed because something important is missing. It could be a feeling of tension, it might be a doubtful voice tone.

These signals are extremely useful; they are a way of tapping into your unconscious intuition in a way that we usually neglect.

You can use the signals in your sport:

■ before a match
■ when deciding on tactics for a race or game
■ when testing your commitment for a game
■ in any decision in the middle of a game where you have time to pause for a moment and check your intuition

But why confine such a useful tool to sport alone? You can use it whenever you have any important decision to make.

What should you do if you feel incongruent? First thank your intuition for warning you. You may not know exactly what reservations you have, but you have them and it is better to deal with them than run ahead regardless. Ask yourself what needs to be different for you to be able to go ahead congruently. Then relax for a moment and listen. It is surprising how often an answer will come that makes sense but that you had not thought of before.

Here are a few reasons why you might be incongruent:

- First you could need more information about the circumstances. The answer to this is simple: find out what you need to know. Where are the blank spots in your knowledge?
- Secondly, you might have all the information you need but be unsure what exactly to do. This is where you can use mental imagery to try out possibilities in the safety of your own mind before doing them in real life.
- Thirdly, you may know what to do but doubt your skill to do it. This is a different level altogether. You need to practise those skills that you need.
- Fourthly, you may have the skill but do not believe you can succeed right now. You may lack the confidence or you may find that the action is really not as important as you thought it was and is not worth doing. This is where the work you did in Chapter 2 about beliefs will be very useful.
- Lastly, you may have enough information, know what to do, be sure of your skill and feel confident, yet somehow it's not really 'you'. At a deep level it does not fit with your identity.

All the emotions, states and muscle memory of playing in the zone are stored in your unconscious. You can never *consciously* analyse what goes on when you are playing your best at the time, because as soon as you do, you are no longer in the zone. So you have to analyse the memory afterwards. How can you get to the real living feelings? By using an unconscious review. The way into the zone is to mobilize your unconscious resources.

Exercise 23: Reviewing Unconscious Resources

Find a time when you can be alone and relax for a few minutes. Lie or sit back and get comfortable. Let all the muscles in your body relax and let your mind drift for a few minutes. Do not try and think of anything but let your mind move where it pleases. Imagine that you are an intrepid explorer in a dark cave with a small torch. You are shining the torch around, almost at random, noticing the rock formations and any objects that are there. You are looking for treasure.

1   Let your mind wander to any occasions when you played very well and were in the zone or flow state. Don't try and think of any but let your mind play with the thought. Ask the deeper part of your mind to review all of those occasions and to let you know when it has finished by giving you the congruence signal. You may remember some times consciously or you may not, it does not matter. Let your mind drift – it doesn't matter if you feel sleepy, or even doze off for a few minutes.

2   When you have finished, ask your unconscious to review all the coaching, preparation and experience you enjoyed before those great games. Ask the unconscious to give you the congruence signal when it is complete.

3   When you have done that, ask your unconscious to review those great games and explore all the ways to ensure that you are in the right state to play another great game like those. Ask it to give you the congruence signal when you are ready.

4   When you are ready, ask your unconscious mind to review all the ways it has discovered and give you the congruence signal when it is ready to implement any or all those ways to play another great game.

5   When you have finished, open your eyes, stretch and get ready for another great game.

If you play a team sport, you can also ask the deeper part of your mind to review all the times when you played well as a team player. This is much too complicated to try to do consciously – you were responding moment to moment to the other team members and you did not know in advance what would happen. Go through the same process with the team games.

Be patient in this exercise. The zone is worth waiting for. If you do not get a signal that any step is complete after a reasonable time, go on to the next step and start the process from the beginning another time. Even if the process is incomplete, you will have reviewed some of the examples.

This is a wonderful exercise that benefits from practice. You are marshalling your unconscious resources to put you into the zone and forming a good relationship with your unconscious processes. That is bound to improve your game.

Some of the exercises in this chapter are not very easy to do on your own, but an audiotape of these exercises is available that makes them very easy to follow *(see Training and Resources, page 196)*. You can relax, listen to the audiotape and pause the tape when you need time to process. When you are ready to continue, switch the tape on again. Alternatively, you can make your own audiotape by recording the instructions.

You cannot force your way into the zone. It is like a shy friend that you have to invite into your house. All you can do is make your home a comfortable place and make your friend welcome.

The final paradox of the flow state is that the quickest way in is to *stop* doing things – clear away the distractions that prevent you being there. How you deal with distractions is crucial to the quality of your concentration and your game. You also need to deal with the distractions that might get in the way of your mental rehearsal. Dealing with distractions is the subject of the next chapter.

REFERENCES

Czikszentmihalyi, M., *Flow: The Psychology of Happiness*, Rider, 1992
Gallwey, T., *The Inner Game of Tennis*, Random House, 1974
Herrigel, E., *Zen and the Art of Archery*, Pantheon Books, 1953
Nideffer, R. M., *The Inner Athlete*, Crowell, 1976

CHAPTER FOUR SUMMARY

Our level of play varies from game to game:

The pits are the worst – everything goes wrong.
The zone is the best – everything goes right.

Being in the zone is the ultimate goal for athletes. It is where they play at their absolute best. The zone is sometimes called the 'flow state'. When you are in the zone:

- There is no trying.
- The game feels easy.
- There is no thinking.
- You are completely in the present moment.
- Time seems to stand still.

Concentration

Concentration is a process of paying attention. You focus on what is important and delete other things. The important questions are:

What are you paying attention to?
What are the qualities of your attention?

The three principles of concentration:

1   Concentration is natural and easy. You do it all the time, selectively paying attention to what is important to you and blotting out the rest.
2   What distracts you has to be a significant change, so you can control distractions by what you define as significant.
3   You cannot try to eliminate distractions, you can only focus on what is important to you and they will disappear naturally.

Concentration has focus: either broad or narrow.
Concentration has direction: either outwards or inwards.

There are four main ways to concentrate your attention:

1 outwards with a broad focus
2 outwards with a narrow focus
3 inwards with a broad focus
4 inwards with a narrow focus

These are four ways of concentrating and they are also four styles of playing.

Each of these styles has strengths and weaknesses.

Ideally you need to give attention in a fluid and balanced way, moving between the four styles depending on the state of the game.

Distractions are when your focus of attention is not in the right place at the right time.

You need to identify the critical points in your sport and determine what sort of concentration style you need and where you need to focus your attention.

The styles of concentration are different states of mind and you can set up associations that will reliably take you into these states. These associations are known as 'triggers' or 'anchors'.

Setting up anchors involves building a ritual that helps you achieve the concentration you need, mentally rehearsing it so it becomes automatic and practising it at every opportunity in the game.

You also need to set up an anchor to take you into a neutral state when you are angry or upset in the game.

The two great enemies of concentration are anxiety and fatigue.

The Unconscious

The paradox of the zone is that the moment you analyse it, you come out of it. When you are in the zone you are unselfconscious.

Your conscious mind cannot deal with the speed and precision needed in sport – you have to rely on your unconscious resources. To achieve the flow state you need to be in harmony with your unconscious process, trust yourself and let yourself go in order to achieve the state of 'no mind'.

To get in harmony with your unconscious resources:

- Treat your body well and take care of yourself.
- Listen and pay attention to your feelings and signals about what is the best thing to do.

Congruence is the state when you feel in harmony with your unconscious.

Incongruence is when you have reservations, when you feel uncomfortable without knowing why.

You can become more intuitive and learn to recognize your signals for congruence and incongruence and use them in your sport:

- before a match
- when deciding on tactics for a race or game.
- in testing your commitment for a game
- in making any decision in the middle of a game where you have time to pause and check your intuition

When you feel incongruent it could be that:

- You need more information about the circumstances.
- You do not know exactly what to do.
- You doubt your skill to do what is needed.
- You do not believe you can succeed right now – you may lack the confidence or the situation may not be important to you.
- You do not think it fits with your identity.

The way into the flow state is to:

- review and utilize unconscious resources
- remove distractions

Dealing with Distractions

Concentration gets you into the zone and lets you play at your best. Distractions interfere with your concentration and take you out of the zone. When you are fit and skilled, distractions are the final and most elusive enemies. These enemies are hard to defeat because when they appear your first thought is to try to ignore them, but if you do so you will never understand how they operate.

The army of distractions has three principal types of soldier, one for each sense – visual, auditory and kinesthetic:

- foveal vision (visual)
- internal dialogue (auditory)
- unnecessary muscle tension (kinesthetic)

We will deal with each in turn.

Foveal Vision

There is a spot in the centre of the retina of each eye called the *fovea centralis*. It has the greatest concentration of cells, called cones, that are sensitive to colour and bright light. When you stare at an object, that is where you automatically try to focus the image; it gives the best definition. This is foveal vision. The other sort of cells in the eye are called rods and are concentrated at the edges of the retina. They are sensitive to light, darkness and movement.

Foveal vision is good for focused narrow external attention, but not for the kind of free-flowing attention that is needed to play sport. We generally use it for conscious, analytical, language-based, so-called 'left-brained' thinking (because the left hemisphere of the brain is the part that carries out this sort of thinking). Sport needs spatial awareness and a more wide-ranging attention to movement. These are so-called 'right-brained' skills, being processed in the right cerebral hemisphere of the brain.

The type of vision you need in sport is *peripheral vision*. 'Peripheral' means towards the edge or on the boundary. Peripheral vision means having a wide visual field, expanding the boundary so you can see more. It uses the cells at the edge of the retina (the rods) which are more sensitive to movement. Peripheral vision is like a hawk high in the sky, surveying the ground, focusing on nothing in particular, but seeing everything. When it sees its prey, it focuses in and swoops down.

Peripheral vision is much better than foveal vision for tracking movement. You can easily test this. Stand at the side of a road and watch the cars speed by. Stare at an oncoming car and see how accurately you can judge its speed and how long it will take before it passes you. Now look away and watch another car from the corner of your eye. This way it is much easier to judge the speed. If you want to cross a busy road, use peripheral vision to gauge the traffic!

Peripheral vision is characteristic of the flow state because it engages the unconscious process. It is almost impossible to achieve that magic state of 'no mind' when you are staring at something with foveal vision, because foveal vision immediately engages the conscious mind, giving a signal to your brain that says, 'Wake up! I want you to think about this in detail.'

Exercise 24: Developing Peripheral Vision

This exercise will open your eyes to peripheral vision.

Place the tips of your index fingers together in front of you about a foot away at eye height, as if you were starting to pray. Now keep your right index finger steady and keep looking at it. Imagine your fingers are part of a circle that extends all the way round your head. Slowly move your left index finger following the circle towards your left ear. Keep looking straight at your right index finger in front of you all the time. Keep moving your left hand until you can't see your left finger any more. Now see where your left index finger has moved to – somewhere level with your ear.

Now do the same little exercise keeping your left index finger in front of you and moving your right index finger off to your right until you cannot see it any more. Your total field of vision lies between the limits you have just found – from ear to ear – far wider than the field you normally use. Most of the time we confine ourselves to about a third of our possible visual field because we rely too heavily on foveal vision.

Here's another short exercise you can do with peripheral vision.

- Start by staring intently at something in front of you. Look at it in detail. Notice how the focus of your eyes affects the way you think.
- Now, without moving your head, let your field of vision expand. Be aware of what lies beyond your central focus. Notice how opening your vision also gives you a sense of opening your mind and having more space both in your mind and outside. There is space all around you, but you won't use it unless you are aware of it. You don't lose the central focus when you use peripheral vision – there is no need to stare into infinity!
- Now focus back on the object in front of you, while keeping the sense of awareness of what lies beyond.

You can use the power of peripheral vision immediately in your sport:

- *Before you compete.*
  Peripheral vision is an important part of mental rehearsal. When you use imagery to prepare for an event make sure you are visualizing as if using peripheral vision. When you arrive at the venue, look around at the whole place before the game begins. Imagine you are taking it all in through your eyes and that the space belongs to you. Let yourself expand and fill the space. It's all yours. Now focus on one part of it, but keep that expanded awareness through your peripheral vision.
- *During the game.*
  Whenever you have an opportunity, expand your vision. Link it to words like 'wider' or 'more'. This small action will have big results.

Internal Voices

Most of us have internal conversations. They are a useful part of thinking, but they do not belong in a match. The zone or flow state is quiet. When you are there you will hear external sounds clearly, but there is rarely an inner voice to disturb the inner calm and silence. Internal voices are distractions, they are the chatter of the conscious mind trying to grab your attention. If they succeed, then you will be caught in an internal narrow focus of attention – the last place you want to be in a match.

Internal voices are a potent distraction and they can take many guises. They may ask you if you left the computer on when you went out or whether you closed all the windows. They may chatter about the venue, the equipment, the referee and officials. They may have something to say about the spectators. Worst of all, they may tell you that you are going to lose and your opponents are much too good for you or start berating you for making a mistake or for not playing well. It is surprising how many mistakes come in pairs. One is the genuine mistake; the second comes from the player being distracted by their internal self-criticism.

Why are internal voices so distracting? Because the auditory sense is at a loose end while the other senses are completely taken up paying attention to the game. During a match you need to turn your attention outwards to what you see. So, what you see won't distract you unless it catches your attention and holds it. A golfer may see the rough he wants to avoid, but that is only distracting if he starts to obsess about it and that usually starts with an internal voice. The rough is important and not distracting in itself, only *thoughts* about it will be distracting. Pain may be a distraction, but often during a game we are able to over-ride pain and deal with it. Emotions may also be distracting but usually in the heat of the game, the exertion and effort leave no room for them. (We will deal with anxiety in the next chapter.) The sense of hearing is much less crucial in a game. It is underused and that leaves a lot of room for internal voices.

What can we do about this self-talk? To begin with, there is a difference between hearing a voice and listening to it. Listening means you are giving it your attention. Attention gives power. So, the obvious advice is 'Don't listen', but that is too facile. It is also negative. What will you listen to instead? You need to listen to something else to drown out your inner voice. That way you might still hear the voice but it won't have the same power. So listen instead to the external sounds. Golfers can listen to the wind in the trees or the sound of their footsteps. Tennis players can pay attention to the sound the ball makes as it bounces and hits their racquet. Footballers can pay attention to the sound of the other players, the thud of the ball on the ground or the shouts of the spectators.

You can also drown out the voice by repeating a word or phrase to yourself. This acts like a mantra, blocking the distracting internal voice. Pick a word that expresses what you want to do, perhaps 'focus' or 'go' or 'calm'. Because your mantra is repetitive and either encouraging or neutral, it will not distract you. The purpose of the mantra is only to block the voice. When that is done, you want to be silent inside again.

The worst distractions are the internal voices that criticize you and sap your confidence with negative thoughts. These usually come in three main varieties:

- fears and anxiety about what could go wrong (but hasn't yet)
- self-criticism
- general negative self-talk, for example about how badly the match is going and how you might lose it

Negative self-talk is one of the enemies that stop you getting into the zone. As always, we shall apply the principle of getting to know your enemies first in order to defeat them. The next exercise will help you understand this one better.

Exercise 25: Analysing Internal Dialogue

Part 1

When do you typically engage in negative self-talk?
Is there any particular event or experience that triggers it, like a mistake, miscalculation or bad decision?
How does the self-talk affect you?
How long does it last?

Think back to some specific times where you were distracted by self-talk.

What were the words?
Whose voice was it? (Usually it's your voice, but for some athletes, it will be the voice of their coach or even their parents!)
What sort of tone did the voice use?

Whereabouts does it come from (for example, does it seem come to come from the front, one side, or the back of your head)?
How loud is it?
Is there any other important quality you notice?

At the end of this part of the exercise you will have the critical submodalities of the distracting internal dialogue.

Part 2

Now *keep the words exactly the same*, but experiment changing the submodalities.

Change the voice tone so it sounds like Donald Duck. Add some circus music. Make the voice sexy. Play and explore – it's all yours, you can do what you like to it. What sort of difference can you make?

Change the direction of the voice. Switch it between the left and right side. Hear it from the front and then put it behind you. Which feels most comfortable?

What difference does it make when you move it further away?

Make it softer. Then try it louder. What difference does that make?

Who do you think is talking? If it sounds like you then imagine someone has taken your voice and is using it without permission.

What might they look like?

Put a face and a body to the voice. A disembodied voice is harder to deal with than an image of a real critic. Some athletes I know make a ridiculous character. They imagine a mean little man, spindly and unfit, rubbing his hands together. They give him a clown's red nose, funny big shoes and a green face. Make the character as absurd as you like, then instead of paying attention to what this idiot says you can just laugh at them and carry on.

If you can do all this then you do have control over the voice. A voice that was loud in your right ear becomes quite different if you make it high and squeaky two yards away on your left. Set this all up beforehand in one of your imagery practices. You will immediately take some of the power out of the voice. Then if the voice pipes up in the game, you will know what to do immediately.

Now listen to the words.

They may be abusive. The voice may call you names when you make a mistake. It may make you feel bad by telling you what a stupid mistake you made and what an idiot you are.

Have you ever thought how strange this is? The voice is yours and it's insulting you! You wouldn't stand for that if someone else did it. And if a teammate made the same mistake, you wouldn't abuse them in quite the same way. It doesn't help to persecute yourself over a mistake and it only makes it worse if you get angry with yourself for persecuting yourself.

Brad Gilbert, the well known American tennis coach, has a great quote. He says, 'When you beat yourself up during a match, you have doubled the number of people trying to defeat you.'

What exactly does the voice say? Does it say, '*You* are stupid...' or does it say, '*I* am stupid...'? Each has a different effect. 'I am stupid' is more immediate, it makes the criticism harder to deal with. But *you* are not stupid, you made a mistake. That's behaviour and does not make you a stupid person. Nor does it make you any less skilful in the future. You'll need to deal with that mistake later through practice or mental rehearsal, but there is nothing that you can do now to change it. You just have to drop the criticism and refocus.

One great technique is to visualize the mistake as some kind of rubbish that you can drop or stamp on. Tennis players can visualize the mistake as a punctured tennis ball. They imagine picking it up and throwing it or hitting it as far away as possible. I know golfers who visualize a mistake as a piece of rubbish on the course. They imagine dropping it in a handy bin. A footballer imagines the mistake as a brightly coloured beach ball which he kicks as hard as he can out of the ground, watching it sail over the heads of the crowd.

Another good technique is to imagine writing down the mistake on a piece of paper using a few key words. Then imagine putting it in a filing cabinet marked 'To be looked at LATER' and closing the drawer. After the game, you imagine opening the filing cabinet and sifting through the mistakes of the day. You decide whether they need any further action and how you can ensure that you do not repeat the same mistake.

Chapter 7 has a process for dealing with mistakes after the game (see page 161). Here is a simple exercise for dealing with mistakes during the game.

Exercise 26: Dealing with Errors

1 If you make a mistake and get angry or upset, use your neutral
   anchor *(see page 101)* to calm yourself.
2 Decide what you want to do with the mistakes. Think of a suitable
   image like a filing cabinet, basket or waste bin – somewhere you
   can park the mistakes so that they won't bother you now but are
   there for you to retrieve later.
3 Then, as soon as you have a pause, quickly imagine what you
   wanted to happen instead of the mistake. *Do not think about the
   mistake again! You will only mentally rehearse it!* Instead, see the
   perfect shot, the excellent kick or the wonderful stroke that you
   intended. This rapidly deals with the mistake so it does not distract
   you and you can still learn from it after the game.

Let the mistake go, it's over, there is no way you can turn back the clock
and unmake it. Pay attention, though, if you keep making the same sort
of mistake – that shows you need to improve your technique in crucial
areas. You can deal with those evaluations after the game.

Now listen more closely to what the self-critical voice is saying. It may
be an armchair critic. Critics have a favourite vocabulary including
words that imply rules like 'should' and 'shouldn't', 'must' and 'must-
n't', 'have to' and 'can't'. Does your internal voice use these words?
Does it say, 'You *should* have done so and so. . .' or 'You *must* play
better. . .'?

This critical talk is useless. It makes you feel worse because it does
not offer any alternative, it just tells you what you already know. When
you hear these sorts of words, change them. Replace 'I should. . .' and
its equivalents with 'I can. . .' So 'I *should* play better' becomes 'I *can*
play better', which is much more empowering.

Try the change out for yourself. Say to yourself, 'I *should* play
better.' Notice how that makes you feel. Most people feel a little resent-
ful and rebellious.

Now say to yourself, 'I *can* play better.' Again, notice how that
makes you feel. Most people feel this is more neutral – just a statement
(unless you give it a voice tone that implies you're deliberately slacking).

The next stage is to say, 'I *will* play better.'

And finally, at the first possible opportunity, 'I *am* playing better.'
Here's the full sequence:

Figure 5.1: Changing critical talk

A simple word change makes a big difference.

The armchair critic may also be full of negatives like 'You *shouldn't*
do that again' or 'I *mustn't* make that mistake again.' It's the same sort
of language, but now it's in the negative and that makes it worse.
Change the words immediately to 'I *won't* do that again.' And then file
the error in your mental filing cabinet to be looked at later or, if it was a
one-off mistake, just throw it away.

Sometimes your internal voice is actually hypnotizing you into mistakes, for example: 'Don't do that again!' Leave out the first word and
what do you have? '*Do that again!*' This is important because your
unconscious does not process negatives. It hears the embedded command
and may act on it – another reason why positive self-talk is so vital.

Chess players are trying to get their game recognized as a sport
(who says sports have to be physically tiring?) so I feel I can tell a chess
story. In an important chess match, a World Championship qualifying
tournament, many years ago, one of the players protested that his opponent had hired a hypnotist to sit in the front row and cast baleful
glances in his direction when he was trying to think. He found this very
distracting and believed the hypnotist was mentally weakening him and
aiding his opponent. When you engage in negative self-talk, it's like
having a hypnotist on the sidelines whispering negative commands.

Why does the voice say anything? Why can't it be quiet?

There has to be some purpose behind the voice, even though it nags and distracts you. Think of it as a very bad coach who needs educating. The positive purpose of a coach and a critic is to help you improve. Their intention is golden, although their methods may be idiotic; underneath their words they are really trying to help you. How would you educate a bad coach?

You have to tell them to find another way to motivate you. What they are doing isn't working. We have already talked about changing the voice tone and some of the phrases to make the coach more positive. What the critical coach is doing is making two fundamental mistakes. The first is telling you about negatives – what you mustn't do, what might go wrong. This not only distracts you, it also makes you picture what you want to avoid. Secondly, the coach is telling you at the wrong time. The right time is after the game, not in the middle of it.

When you are in the midst of a game don't fight the distracting voices. Instead, focus more on what you want to happen. Have you ever taken your date to a party or a pub where there's a lot of noise? Everybody is talking at once, maybe there's a juke box in the corner spewing out last century's hits at a volume that sets the glasses shaking and loosens the fillings in your teeth. At first it's very difficult to talk. But you want to talk, you want to get to know your date, so you pay attention to them, you learn to pick out their voice from the hubbub. After a while the noise seems less loud and does not bother you so much because you are paying attention to someone important. If you can do that in a pub, you can do it in a game. Focus on what's important and the noise will recede into the background. As time passes, you may not even notice it.

Muscle Tension

Now we come to the third enemy of peak performance – unnecessary muscle tension. To play at your best, you need a balance of tension and relaxation. You need some tension, otherwise you would collapse in a heap, but only enough to play the game. Any extra just gets in the way.

There's a word that nearly always brings extra tension in its wake. That word is 'try'. Think of doing something in your sport – hitting or kicking the ball, making a pass, accelerating the pace. Now think of 'trying' to do the same action. Trying is a gritted-teeth, vein-popping, buttock-clenching word, conjuring effort and difficulty.

Luckily, 'trying' only exists in language. It does not exist in the real world. Do this little mind experiment.

Reach up and touch your nose. Easy.
Now don't touch your nose. Easier still.
Now 'try' to touch your nose.

What's the difference between that and the first two? In the real world, you either do something or you do not. Trying is only in the mind; it implies the action is difficult and needs effort. I suggest you remove 'try' from your sporting vocabulary. You will eliminate a lot of unnecessary tension straightaway.

Using peripheral vision will also reduce muscle tension automatically, especially around the eyes and forehead. Too much foveal vision can give you a headache because of the muscle tension. Too much muscle tension anywhere in your body can make that part of your body extra tired after the game. The more muscles you tense, the more energy you use, and if you don't need the muscles then you are simply wasting energy that could be put to much better use.

You may have been unlucky enough to 'choke' or break down in a match. You can always tell when this happens to athletes, you see their shoulders sag and they do a lot of staring at the ground. You see it in tennis matches, boxing matches, even football matches when the whole team suddenly takes on an air of defeat.

Choking is one way of describing this breakdown and it is fascinating that most of the synonyms for choking imply some kind of unwanted body tension. What does choking mean – literally? It means tensing throat muscles and having difficulty breathing. We also say that someone's game has 'broken down' or 'fallen apart'. These are wonderful metaphors and often point to exactly what is happening. NLP takes language literally because language reflects our thought process, and our thought process affects our body, how we feel and which muscles we tense and relax.

What metaphor do you use when your game fails and you give up?

Metaphors of Failure

Here are some ways that we talk about losing. They all imply poor body use and unwanted tension.

'He choked at a critical point...'
'She froze...'
'Their game is cracking up...'
'His game has just broken down...'
'Her game has fallen apart...'
'He's suddenly lost it...'
'Their play has taken a nosedive...'
'He blew up at the final stage...'
'Her game has collapsed...'
'Their game has really gone down...'

A sad litany of phrases. What do you do if you feel that one of these is happening to you? The remedy often lies in the words themselves:

■ If you think of failure as 'choking', remember to breathe and relax your throat.
■ If it seems as though you 'freeze', relax as many muscles as possible (without falling over!) and imagine a great warmth engulfing you.
■ If you think of your game as breaking down or collapsing, imagine 'pulling yourself together'. Imagine bringing all your resources and feelings into the centre of your solar plexus.
■ If you think of your game 'going down' or 'taking a nosedive', look up and relax the muscles in your neck and face.

Whatever metaphor you use, just reverse it and you will get exactly the resource you need to reverse the process.

These phrases describe the sorry final stages of a longer process – these sorts of collapses do not come out of the blue. When you use the other mental tools – mental rehearsal, anchors and ways to centre yourself and concentrate – you will find that you will never get to this point at all.

Time Distortion

When you are in the zone or the flow state, you are fully in the present moment. In that moment, time seems to stand still, and it's all yours. Athletes who have been in the zone say how they seem to have plenty of time to do whatever they want. Tennis players and golfers see the ball as big as a balloon; they can't miss. Runners say that everything seems to happen in slow motion, footballers that everyone else seems to run through treacle while they run on air.

This sort of time distortion may seem a strange phenomenon, but time distortion actually happens all the time. Have you ever watched a kettle boil? Were you ever asked to be quiet for a whole minute as a child? When you pay attention to the passing of time, especially if you are not enjoying yourself, then it drags its feet like a fat boy on a rugby field. Museums always distort time for me. When I was a child I used to believe that they were not only full of old things, but that they also ran on old time, which was a lot slower than modern time. One of the longest hours in my life was going round a foreign museum with some relatives when I was seven years old. I wanted to go and play, but I had to do my duty. I am sure they enjoyed it (they were a lot older than I was), but the only way I could keep sane was to grade exhibits by points of boredom and cast imaginary bets as to whether the next exhibit would be as boring as the last. There was a clock in every room and I was sure that all of them had stopped.

You can also accelerate time – you must have seen a film or television show that so absorbed you that the time flew by. You 'woke up' and the clock said an hour had gone, but it seemed like only an instant. Computer games are particularly good at stealing time. Start a computer game and you may become so absorbed that hours can pass unnoticed.

So, the clock gives you social time, objective time, but we all experience time differently depending on what is happening. We have all had experience of 'fast time' and 'slow time'. Time does not 'really' speed up or slow down, of course, it just seems that way. Your *perception* of time is what matters.

There is a superb science-fiction novel by Alfred Bester called *The Stars my Destination*. The hero, Gully Foyle, has had a special operation to enhance his nervous system. When he presses his tongue against his upper incisors it triggers special neural circuits and

accelerates his body to five times normal speed. He then experiences
the outside world as slowed down to a fifth of its normal speed, so for
him everything is happening in extreme slow motion, although he can
move normally. People seem to float languorously about. Colours shift
towards infra red and sound becomes a deep rumble, like a tape playing
too slowly. To the rest of the world Gully Foyle looks like a blur of
movement. When he wants to return to normal, he presses his tongue
against the back of his top incisors again.

Wouldn't that capability be useful in sport? The ball would slow
right down, your opponents would seem to move in slow motion. It *is*
possible – without the operation. Your brain can do it. All you need is
to find the switch. Here are some exercises that will help you put the
world into s-l-o-w time.

Exercise 27: Fast and Slow Motion Pictures

Pick one of your favourite films. Sit down, relax and imagine the film
beginning.

Imagine the frames at their normal speed and then speed them up.
See the action go faster and faster. You can do this easily if you imagine
watching the film on video. Just push the fast forward button. The actors
rush up and down with quick jerky movements. If you could hear the
sounds, their voices would be high pitched and squeaky, the music
would go *prestissimo*. Watch as much of the film as you like in this way.
You might make it go even faster than the fast forward video speed. In a
few minutes you could watch the whole film.

Now, as you watch the film, start slowing it down. Slow it down until it
is at normal speed. It seems to be going slower than usual, doesn't it? That is
because our perception of speed is affected by what we are used to. You
have probably driven onto a motorway and accelerated up to 70 miles an
hour. That seems fast after 30 miles an hour. Then you cruise along and get
used to the higher speed. Your reactions have to be faster because everything moves quicker. When you come off the motorway you slow down on
the slip road and suddenly you seem to be crawling along, but the
speedometer may be showing 45 miles an hour. What has happened is that
you became accustomed to the faster speed and your reactions are set for
that faster speed. This is the 'motorway slip road effect'. We will use it later.

Now wipe the screen and rewind the tape. Start the film again from the beginning, but this time imagine the frames going very slowly. A film is made of a number of different frames and they are speeded up until the action seems continuous. All you have to do is imagine that the projector is running more and more slowly... Watch as the characters move ... so slowly... They open their mouths and their voices are incredibly deep ... and ... slow ... like an an-i-mal g-r-o-w-l-i-n-g.

Exercise 28: Exploring 'Fast Time'

When you play you want to be in fast time, so your opponents seem slow and you have plenty of time to counter them.

Remember back to a pleasant time when everything seemed to slow down. *Don't pick a bad time when you were bored!* Be back in your pleasant time. What is it like?

Go through the submodalities of how you perceive the world when it seems to be moving slowly:

What do you see?
What is the quality of your pictures?
Do you see brighter colours?
What is the range of your vision?
Listen to any sounds.
What are the qualities of the sounds?
Is your inner voice silent?
Do outside sounds seem louder or softer?
What sort of feeling do you have in your body?
Whereabouts is it?
Is the feeling warm or cool?
How large is it?

Write down your critical submodalities of fast time – how your brain codes fast time. You can use these submodalities to make it easier to enter fast time when you want to *(see the example below)*.

EXPERIENCE OF FAST TIME – CRITICAL SUBMODALITIES (EXAMPLE)

Visual Submodalities	Auditory Submodalities	Kinesthetic Submodalities
Colour seems to be less intense, more muted.	Sounds seem louder and seem to echo more than usual.	Warm and heavy feeling in the body centred in the solar plexus. The feeling is about the size of a football.
Slower movement of pictures.	Sound is clear. No internal dialogue	
Pictures seem more three dimensional – they seem to have a greater depth.		
Wide-angle vision.		

Other comments:
I notice far more detail than usual.
I am in the present moment concentrating on where I am and what is happening now.
There is little awareness of what has just happened or what I want to happen next.

This example is that of a tennis player I helped to enter fast time. He picked an experience of a pleasant evening when he was relaxing and time seemed to go very slowly.

Your submodalities of fast time will be unique to you, but I have found some common qualities of fast time in my work with athletes:

■ They are very much in the present moment.
■ They are using peripheral vision – they have a wide angle of vision.
■ There is no internal dialogue.

These qualities hardly come as a surprise because they are characteristic of the flow state and in the flow state time seems to go more slowly.

Fast time is not something you can will yourself into. It is like being in the zone – once you try to do it with your conscious mind, you come out of it. Fast time is an altered state and to get into it you have to use imagery and mental rehearsal.

Exercise 29: Getting into 'Fast Time'.

■ *Mental rehearsal before the game.*
Relax and let your mind drift for a few minutes. Now imagine yourself at your next game. Look around and see the surroundings, listen to any sounds that are there, feel energized and ready to play. Now give that scene your individual submodalities of fast time. In the above example, you would make the colours less intense and slow down any movement you see (but not *your* movements!) You would make the scene appear to have a greater depth and you would open your angle of vision so you are using your peripheral vision. Then you would imagine the sounds a little louder and give them an echo. Next you would imagine a warm, heavy feeling in the pit of your stomach. Make sure you are associated in the picture, looking out through your own eyes.
Spend a few minutes enjoying that experience of fast time. Then imagine yourself starting to play your game. Everything seems to be moving slowly on the outside so you have all the time you need to react. Then create an anchor for that state. (Maybe by touching the back of your upper incisors with your tongue?) The word 'S-L-O-W' would work well. Say it slowly. Anchors need to fit the state they are anchoring – a fast, excited voice tone is not going to help you go into fast time.

■ *At the game.*
Before you start playing look around and deliberately try to speed up what you see. Imagine you are seeing a video going faster than usual. Then click back into ordinary vision. Events will seem to have slowed down by contrast – the 'motorway slip road effect'.
Now use your anchor (for example, say 'S-L-O-W' to yourself) and briefly transform the scene with the submodalities of your fast time. Don't think about it. Don't start looking around and ask yourself whether it has worked or not. Just get on with the match.

Whenever you want fast time, use the anchor and then go straight into the game.

Remember that like all anchors and states of mind, this one takes time to establish. And like the zone, it is like a very shy friend. You have to keep inviting it, making it welcome and not trying to insist that it visits you. This way, you will find that both your shy friends will visit you with increasing frequency.

REFERENCES

Alfred Bester, *The Stars my Destination,* SF masterworks edition, Millennium, 1999

CHAPTER FIVE SUMMARY

Concentration

Your concentration can be broken by distractions. A distraction is something that takes your attention away from the game in the present moment.

There are three enemies of concentration, one for each sense:

- foveal vision – focusing on an object directly and consciously
- internal dialogue – when you talk to yourself
- unnecessary muscle tension

The corresponding resources are:

- *Peripheral vision*

  Peripheral vision links more with unconscious processes.
  It is better for judging speed and movement.
  It is characteristic of the flow state or the zone.

- *Inner silence*
  Internal dialogue is either self-criticism, unnecessary chatter or worry about what could go wrong. You can deal with internal dialogue by:

- listening to sounds in the outside world
- using a repetitive word like a mantra to drown out the internal dialogue
- understanding when it happens and what causes it
- exploring the critical submodalities (e.g. voice tone, direction) and changing them
- visualizing a ridiculous person saying the words so they become laughable
- developing a ritual to 'throw away' mistakes at the time, so you can deal with them later

- changing phrases like 'I should play better...' to 'I can play better', then to 'I will play better', then to 'I am playing better'
- stopping phrases that act as negative embedded commands
- understanding what the voice's positive intention is and finding another way to satisfy it

- *Muscle balance*

All metaphors of failure like 'choking' imply muscle tension and often give clues to what you can do to counteract them.
The word 'try' often conjures up unnecessary tension by implying effort and difficulty.

Time Distortion

Our perception of time is changeable. This happens naturally and we can utilize it in sport.

When in the flow state, time seems to have a different quality. You are in 'fast time' and have plenty of time to make your moves.

Identify the critical submodalities of your own 'fast time' and use them in your games.

Energy and Intensity

Emotional Intensity

I often watch late night television and indulge in hopping idly from channel to channel. There is rarely anything on that I want to watch but I like the variety. It's 'buffet TV' – plenty of small dishes to sample, but no main course in sight. One night I came upon a football match and watched for a few minutes. Players moved, ran, passed and tackled in constant motion like a stylish dance. No one was still. At half time, the experts came on to give their opinions of the match so far. One of these commentators called one of the players a 'thinking player'. This made me laugh because all the players were thinking players – if they weren't thinking, they wouldn't be able to move. There's no movement without thought. You can't see them thinking, however, you can only see the results. I suppose this was what the commentator meant.

By chance my next hop took me to a philosophical discussion. Three people were seated around a table earnestly debating the issues of the day. One asked a question and the other put his hand to his chin and stared into space for several seconds before answering. Another got up and started pacing the floor. I wondered whether a philosophy commentator would call them 'athletic thinkers'. Each person's body was supporting their thinking just as the footballer's thoughts were supporting his movements.

When you are competing it seems there is no time to think but you are thinking all the time. Best-quality play and best-quality thinking comes from body and mind working together harmoniously. And most thinking is taking place unconsciously; you are unaware of it.

This chapter is about controlling your energy and intensity so that you have the right degree of emotional intensity and the right degree of physical energy to play at your best. When you are physically tired, you feel lethargic and mentally slow. When you lack mental energy, confidence and motivation, it is harder to raise the physical energy you need. The effects of too little energy are obvious. Too much energy is also a problem – it can lead to overhitting, wild and irresponsible play, anger, choking and physical injury. How can we play with the right sort of intensity and get the best results for the least effort? What quality of thinking do we need to get the best balance of energy and intensity?

Emotional intensity is translated into physical energy and the sheer physical movements of a game can themselves stir our emotions – footballers get more emotional than chess players, for example, and they are a lot more active. We need to channel our emotions *into the game* rather than ignoring them or letting them spill out. We can perform incredible feats when we push ourselves or are pushed by a coach we respect. You have probably experienced being angry in a game and that anger has given you more energy – you played better, you wanted to win, you wanted to get even. John McEnroe was famous (or infamous) for his temper tantrums on the tennis court. He would argue and shout, and it looked as if he had lost his concentration. Yet he would play the next point beautifully as if nothing had happened. His outbursts probably put off his opponents more than him. McEnroe was unusual. It is not easy to harness emotion to help your game and not hinder it. For every McEnroe there are ten athletes who play worse when they get upset and show their anger. How can we use the energy of emotion? How can we balance our energy? How can we walk the balance between too much emotional and physical intensity and too little?

Here is a summary of the dangers of too little intensity and too much intensity.

ENERGY AND INTENSITY

Too little intensity	Balanced emotional and physical intensity	Too much intensity
low energy		excess muscle tension, especially in the neck and shoulders
lethargy		anger
easily distracted		anxiety
dissociation – feeling 'not all there'		foveal vision
poor motivation		shallow, quick breathing
slower reactions		'butterflies in the stomach'
poor team spirit		choking under pressure
giving way easily under pressure		becoming upset over trivia
difficulty in concentrating		exaggerated reactions to events
too wide a focus of attention		narrow concentration all the time
not caring about the result		trying to win at all costs
defeatism		overwork and effort
feeling tired all the time		feeling exhausted afterwards
feeling dissatisfied with yourself		nausea

'Warming up' is another way of thinking about intensity. It's like heating water. You start with a block of ice – frozen solid, inflexible and uncomfortable to touch. This would be the equivalent of having no energy and intensity – you 'just can't be bothered' with your sport. As you heat the ice, it turns to water and starts to flow, although it is still chilly to the touch. Now the muscles and tendons are becoming warmer and more flexible and you are starting to gain emotional energy and intensity. The physical warmth and the mental warmth or energy build together until you reach the right temperature to play. Your muscles are warm and flexible and you are emotionally committed. In our metaphor of heating water, the water is now comfortably warm – a nice temperature for a shower. But what happens if you keep heating the water? It gets too hot and too uncomfortable. Eventually it boils over and turns to steam. There is only a small temperature range where water is comfortably warm for a shower, and only a small range of emotional and physical intensity where your game is at its best. Go too far and you will 'boil over' or 'lose your cool'.

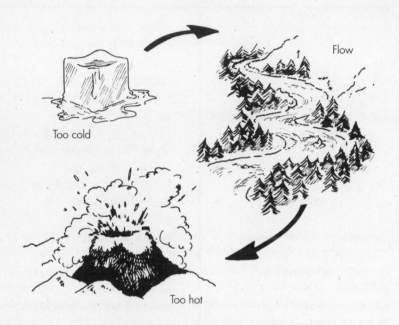

Figure 6.1: Warming up for the game

As far back as 1908 Yerkes and Dobson proposed the relationship between intensity and performance looks like an inverted 'U' *(see Figure 6.2)* and this has been the basis of studies ever since. Performance suffers when you lack intensity. It improves with more intensity, but only up to a point. After that critical point, the top of the 'U' curve, it gets worse again as extra intensity adds nothing to the performance but makes the athlete irritable, distracted and anxious – a good demonstration that if something is good for you, then more is not necessarily better. In terms of our hot water metaphor, the top of the 'U' is where the water temperature is comfortable.

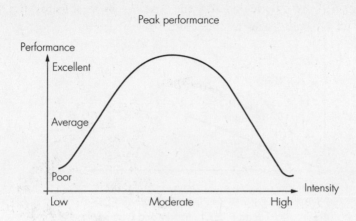

Figure 6.2: Intensity and performance – the inverted 'U' curve

Too high or too low intensity means poor performance. They feel different, but both lead to poor results.

How can we get to the peak of the inverted 'U' curve? How can we get to the comfortable temperature at the top – warmed up just enough to play our best? The answer is not some magical universally applicable energy level. Your ideal energy balance is unique to you and only you can find it, so let's turn the question around and look at what might stop us getting to the top of the 'U' or, once there, send us sliding down the other side.

First, you need to climb up the 'U' curve. Two situations will make this a harder climb than usual: either your opponent seems too easy to defeat and so you don't bother to bring much energy to the game or they seem so superior that you lose heart. In both cases you will struggle in the 'drone zone'.

Secondly, what could cause you to overheat? Feeling angry or upset is the usual reason. The game seems out of control or you are on the receiving end of a bad call by a match official. When the game feels out of control, you may feel out of control as well. This is the 'anxiety zone'. Here energy bubbles up like lava from an exploding volcano and interferes with your concentration. What can you do? Some players direct their anger at the officials, but that only leads to more bad feeling.

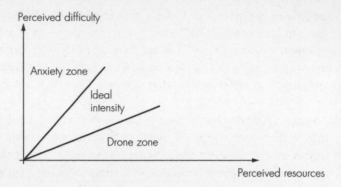

Figure 6.3: Challenge and intensity

Your energy level determines how you see the challenge you face and your ability to cope with it. When we think our resources are far greater than the challenge we are set, then we are likely to enter the drone zone. When we think the challenge is greater than our resources to cope with it, we are most likely to go into the 'anxiety zone'.

Hopes, expectations, focus on past results or future fears will all take you away from where you want to be. Thoughts in the moment are what matter, not grading points, previous results, predicted form or past history. Your ideal performance state is when you are in the present moment.

Whenever we pay attention to the past or future we risk losing our best intensity and energy.

This is the answer to the question of what stops you being in your ideal playing zone. Thinking of the past or future creates hopes, expectations or anxiety that will prevent you climbing the 'U' curve or knock you off the top. For example, if you have easily beaten your opponents previously then it may be harder to summon up energy for a match. You risk being in the drone zone. Even worse, suppose you find yourself in difficulties against a weaker opponent. You might think, 'This is ridiculous! I should be able to beat them. I did before. It looks worse to lose against weaker opposition.' This sort of thinking can tip you into the anxiety zone.

The top of the 'U' curve is the place where past meets future and only the present exists. When you are in the present moment, there are no expectations to distract you and the occasion does not matter. A big occasion can be distracting and make you feel anxious, but if you are in the present moment then all you are thinking of is your next move. The best way to stay in the present moment is to focus your attention outwards and pay attention to what you see, hear and feel on the outside.

You may spend the whole game in the drone zone, balanced intensity zone or the anxiety zone, but usually you move between the three. You may even start the game in the lower reaches of the 'panic zone' if your opponent has a great reputation, the competition is intense and the occasion is important. Then you use your anchors to concentrate, get into a flow state and start playing beautifully. You are winning easily, so you relax, you think you have the match in the bag and drift into the drone zone. Suddenly your opponent starts to play as one inspired. The score evens out, you are neck and neck and the pressure is on. They have the initiative. Now you could find yourself re-entering the panic zone. You might feel tense and start to berate yourself: 'How could I let this happen? I must buckle down and concentrate!' Before you know it, your opponent has pulled ahead and won. The remedy is to stay in the present moment. Play each point, each ball, each part of the game as if that were the most important moment, as if that were the whole game. It makes no difference what the score is. It doesn't matter if you are winning by a long way or losing by a long way, stay completely in the present moment, paying attention not to the score, but to what you have to do *now*.

Get to know how you feel when you are in these different zones. In NLP terms this is called *calibration*. When you know the signs of each zone, you can take action to move out of them if necessary.

You have probably had the experience of feeling a little sluggish and not wanting to exercise or practise when you should. If you follow that thought then you will probably feel even more tired. If you exercise regardless, you will find the energy you thought you did not have. So if you want energy in a game, act energetically! Look up, square your shoulders, move more quickly, make some strong physical movements. Rugby players will often pound themselves or each other with their fists to get psyched up before a match (not hard enough to hurt, however). Energetic activity will make you feel energetic. There are several other ways you can use to energize yourself:

■ *Create and use an anchor for energy.*
Use the process on page 98 to create an energy anchor. Practise it and use it whenever you need energy. Alternatively, you can think of something that makes you angry and this will give you energy. I was playing a game of squash recently and winning fairly easily. I may have drifted a little into the drone zone when there was a disputed call for a let that went in my favour. My opponent clearly did not agree and was furious. He didn't let the anger explode but channelled the energy into his play. He won the next four points with a display of powerful hitting before I woke up to the danger and found some energy of my own to counterattack and win the game.
Here's another example. I worked with an athlete who would visualize the face of someone who had cheated him out of a lot of money whenever he wanted energy. This made him feel angry and determined. Then he dropped the image but kept the energy. He would say to himself, 'Never again!' as an auditory anchor for his new state. You could say 'Energy!' or 'Let's go!' Say these words energetically! A whining internal voice that says, 'Come on, please,' is not going to give you energy.

■ *Instead of saying the words to yourself, you can say or shout them out loud.*
Some teams use rhythmic chanting to 'fire themselves up'. Many squash players I know will shout, 'Come on!' when they need more energy.

■ *Associate.*
When you are in the drone zone, you are likely to be a little dissociated – 'not all there', with 'there' being the balanced intensity zone. To associate, imagine standing beside a blurry double image of yourself. Then step into the image and feel it solidify and become sharp and clear. Come fully into your body, feel your feet on the ground and pay attention to your breathing.

■ *Act 'as if' you have more energy.*
Your body and mind are so closely linked that when you act as if something is true then you start to feel that way. Negative thoughts give signals to the body to act in a negative way. Acting in a

negative way automatically makes it easier to think negatively and you can get into a vicious circle.
When you want to feel something, act as if you already have it!

There will also be times when you have too much energy and you need to ease off and cool down. Here are some suggestions to decrease intensity:

■ *Use imagery.*
  Centre yourself by using calming visualizations.
■ *Broaden your focus of attention, using peripheral vision.*
  Turn your attention outwards. Look at the scene, listen to the sounds in the environment.
■ *Dissociate.*
  Imagine stepping out from your body and seeing it from the outside. Imagine seeing red hot swirls of energy going around inside you. Then gradually make the swirls less red ... gradually change them to orange and then to yellow. Stop when they are the right colour for the energy you want. As you do that, make the swirling energy slow down until it circulates at a comfortable speed. Then imagine stepping back into your body. You can do this routine before a match if you feel tense and nervous.

A lot of physical activity gives you energy, and in games like football and rugby that energy often spills over into confrontation and anger. If you play these sorts of sport, you may find you need to cool down at regular intervals during the game.

Breathing

Breathing happens (thankfully!) all by itself and we usually give it no attention. It adjusts automatically to our level of exertion. However, we can influence our breathing and this is one of the most powerful ways you can change your energy level.

Try this experiment. Hold your breath until you start to feel a little tight in the chest – probably after about 30 seconds. Then breathe out. Do this twice. Notice the sensations. Feel how it makes your shoulders and neck tight, how you may feel a little anxious.

When you are anxious you hold your breath and so holding your breath *makes* you feel anxious for no reason, they are the physical and the mental components of the same experience and they come together. You may also have noticed that the feelings of excitement and anxiety are very similar. Both give you an adrenaline rush in the pit of your stomach. Both bring about physical changes that prepare you for action to meet the unexpected. Both are feelings of anticipation – excitement for something good, anxiety for something bad. Physically, the greatest difference between anxiety and excitement is in the breathing pattern. When you are excited, you breathe deeply. When you are anxious, you tend to hold your breath and breathe shallowly.

Anxiety = Excitement minus breathing

When you breathe quickly and shallowly from the upper part of the chest, you do not completely get rid of the carbon dioxide that accumulates in the lungs. This leads to slightly raised levels of carbon dioxide in the blood, which is the biochemical cause of that heightened feeling of anxiety. You have probably heard people advise 'taking a good deep breath' as the way to stop feeling nervous. That is only half-true and a half-truth can be worse than a lie. A good deep breath gets oxygen into your lungs, but you have to breathe out too!

If you feel anxious before a game, breathe deeply, but take twice as long on the out breath as on the in breath. Count as you breathe – breathe in on 1–2–3, hold for 1–2–3 and then breathe out for a count of 6. Breathe deeply from the diaphragm, the large muscle between your lungs and abdomen. Unless you use the diaphragm, you will restrict your breathing to the smaller area of your upper chest and that is not enough to give you the oxygen your body needs to play well. It seems as if your chest expands at the front when you breathe, but in fact your ribcage expands mostly at the back. You can feel this if you put your hands on either side of your back above your kidneys and breathe in. Compare that expansion to your front upper chest. Your greatest capacity is in the lower part of the lungs.

Here is a simple exercise you can use at any time to balance your energy through your breathing.

Exercise 30: Balancing your Breathing

Part 1

1 Visualize your lungs. Imagine that they are divided into three parts – a bottom section, middle section and top section.

2 Imagine your diaphragm moving down and filling the bottom part of your lungs. Feel your abdomen swell as that part fills up with air, then breathe out.

3 Now do the same with the middle part of your lungs. Your diaphragm will still move but now you should feel the expanse of your chest cavity and feel your ribs raising at the front and back. It helps to hold your sides – put your hands on your hips, as if you were telling someone off, and then move them up the sides of your body as far as they will comfortably go. Breathe out.

4 Now fill the top part of your lungs only, raise your chest and shoulders and breathe out.
Which part had the greatest capacity? Which part had the least capacity?

5 Now fill all three parts of your lungs from the bottom upward in one smooth, fluid motion. Make it easy and effortless and feel you are using your full lung capacity. Then breathe out and relax your shoulders, chest and abdomen as you do. Do this ten times. Afterwards you will feel more relaxed.

Use this exercise as a natural way of relaxing before your imagery practice to prepare your mind for mental rehearsal. You can also use this full, relaxed form of breathing as a neutral anchor, especially if you imagine that you are breathing out the anger and frustrations of the game. Imagine those feelings as some kind of coloured air, maybe red because that is associated with anger. As you breathe out, imagine you are breathing out the red air and with it the anger.

Jackie Stewart, the champion racing driver, used a similar strategy before his Grand Prix races. The day before the race, he said he felt like an overinflated beach ball. He felt as though he was bouncing along as he walked, a little out of control. Over the course of the day, he imagined letting the air out gradually until the tension was just right. At the start of the race, he was famous for being absolutely deadpan. He was completely in balance and in control. I don't know, but I would guess that his breathing when he got into the car before the race was very different from how he was breathing the previous day.

Emotion and Stress

Emotions give us tremendous energy and they can also work against us. Anxiety and nerves before a game make it harder to play well. Performance anxiety or pre-match nerves are a sign of over-intensity.

A game is a challenge. Whenever we are challenged, we react not to the event itself but to our perception of it – what it means to us. For example, imagine walking along in the country and suddenly seeing what you think is a snake out of the corner of your eye. You jump, your heart beats faster, you feel the 'fight or flight' reaction that has been the same for many thousands of years. Then you take a second look and realize it is only a length of rope. You start to calm down, but it was your perception that made you jump, and that is the same whether there is a snake there or not – all that matters is that you think there is a snake.

Your reaction starts in a small part of your brain called the hypothalamus, which is closely connected to the part that controls emotion. The hypothalamus also regulates many of your body's unconscious processes – pulse rate, temperature, breathing and blood pressure. It triggers the release of neurochemicals called beta-endorphins, which are the body's own powerful painkillers that help us to stand pain and discomfort. Beta-endorphins are the reason you can make more physical effort in your sport and also why you don't feel the pain of minor injuries at the time. They help you play on when you are hurt because you do not feel the pain; this is a mixed blessing because playing on usually makes an injury worse.

The flight or fight reaction makes us more alert. The pupils of our eyes dilate to let in more light, our body hair stands erect so we are more sensitive to touch and vibration. Blood flows to the large muscles in the arms and legs and torso and away from internal processes like digestion. Our rate and depth of breathing increase and so does the level of sugar in the blood to provide immediate energy. These are very useful reactions if you need to make a strenuous effort; they are designed to help you exert yourself. In one sense sports competition is a fight, so you want those beta-endorphins, however if the reaction goes on too long or too intensely, it has the opposite effect: you feel stressed, anxious and nervous.

What causes this overreaction before the game? What makes you feel anxious and stressed rather than excited and ready? Your body does not feel anxious for no reason; you have to be creating it in some way. Because it happens *before* the game, you are not responding to the game itself, but to your thoughts about it.

Worry and anxiety are abstract nouns. What do they mean? What are you actually doing when you feel worried or anxious?

First, you think a lot but do very little – there isn't anything you can do. You may worry about events that are completely out of your control (like weather conditions). You may feel as though you have to consciously and totally control everything else, and that is a big burden. When you are anxious you sway between the two extremes – feeling bad about having no control or feeling bad that you must have total control.

Secondly, anxiety is not directed towards a goal. It comes from thinking about what you do *not* want to happen – a disastrous imaginary future that you want to avoid. Thirdly, all this takes place in your mind, there is no reality check because nothing has happened yet. The next exercise is the best way of dealing with performance anxiety and pre-match nerves.

Exercise 31: Dealing with Anxiety before the Game

Part 1: Understanding Anxiety

1   Breathe evenly and deeply. Breathe out for at least the same time as you take to breathe in. As you relax your body, notice where you feel the anxiety.

   Is it in your stomach?
   Your jaw?
   Your neck?

2   As you feel those feelings of anxiety, become aware of the imagery that is going through your mind. What sort of pictures are you making of the game that you will soon be playing?

You may be aware of very little to begin with. Focus on the feelings of anxiety and tension that you have in your body and let an image come from those.

You may find an image that you have every right to be anxious about.

It may be pictures of you doing badly, being laughed at or breaking down. It may be pictures of your parents or coaches scolding you for letting them down. It may be pictures of many spectators, all with unfriendly eyes looking at you and willing you to fail.

Many people get nervous before a performance – public speakers, actors, musicians as well as athletes – and there is usually a similar picture that drives that feeling. They are reacting not to the event itself (it hasn't happened yet), but to imagined possibilities about the event. Sometimes athletes have pictures of equipment breaking down. These pictures are often in full colour, big, close and moving. They are also fully associated, so you are inside them experiencing the situation. When this happens, no wonder you feel anxious!

3   There is usually some self-talk that goes with these pictures. Listen to your internal dialogue. This self-talk is usually of the 'What if...?' variety in an anxious tone of voice:

'What if I am late?'
'What if my arm starts hurting again?'
'What if my sports equipment breaks?'
'What if I lose badly?'

The self-talk and crazy pictures go together and reinforce each other.

This type of anxiety is easy to deal with. Think of it as a skill. You are very good at seeing pictures of events, talking to yourself about them and then having feelings about them. None of these pictures are *true*! You are mentally rehearsing doomsday scenarios. However, you are obviously very good at mental rehearsal – only in this case, it is working against you.

You feel anxious when you mentally rehearse what you don't want to happen and this produces uncomfortable feelings. The natural antidote is positive mental rehearsal when you imagine what you really want and feel good about it.

Part 2: Worry into Planning

You can also turn the worry and anxiety into planning.

1   Start with your internal dialogue. Ask yourself, 'What could go
    wrong?' Then make a list. For example:

    You could be late for the competition
    You could feel ill.
    A key member of the team could be ill or missing.
    You could forget clothing or equipment.
    There could be bad weather or bad conditions.
    You could have a recurrence of an old sports injury.
    You could injure yourself.
    You could play very badly and be dropped from the team.
    You could lose.

    Such a list is endless because there are thousands of ways that
    things could go wrong and only a few in which they go right.

2   The next step is to split the list into two – those things you have
    some degree of control over and those things that you have no
    control over. Remember that control is never absolute. We don't
    even fully control our own bodies, as you know to your cost when
    you get a cold. Here's an example of a control list:

Controllable	Uncontrollable
being late (oversleeping)	being late (external circumstances)
	member of team missing
forgetting clothing or equipment	
	bad weather
	conditions of competition
old sports injury recurring	
injury during the game	
poor performance	
loss of concentration	
lack of fitness	

your opponent has a peak
performance day

There is no point worrying about those things that are outside your
control – you can do nothing about them. For those things that are
in your control, you need to develop a plan and focus on what you
want to happen.

3 Go through each worry in turn and instead of thinking, 'What if this
   happens?' ask, 'What will I do if this were to happen?' This is a
   much more useful question because it dissociates you from the
   events, puts them into a possible future and puts your attention onto
   your positive actions rather than the events themselves. You are now
   causing what you want to happen rather than finding yourself at the
   mercy of events.

4 List the worries again that you have some control over and add
   what you are going to do about them. For example:

Worry	Plan
You could be late for the competition.	Leave half an hour earlier than planned, also have a shortened pre-match warm up routine if necessary.
You could feel ill.	Get a good night's sleep, take extra vitamin C for a few days before.
A key member of the team could be ill or missing.	No control.
You could forget clothing or equipment.	Pack the night before and put in extra gear and back up equipment.
There could be bad weather or bad conditions.	No control.
You could have a recurrence of an old sports injury.	Strap the injury, warm up carefully, be very sensitive to that part of your body. Check with your congruence signal that it is OK to play.

You could injure yourself.	Go through a mental rehearsal for successful performance. Be aware of the physical conditions (e.g. rain) and take extra precautions if necessary.
You could play very badly...	Mental rehearsal, practice, setting anchors, using time distortion.
...and be dropped from the team.	No control.
You could lose...	Positive imagery and good preparation and...
You could win!	

5 Mentally rehearse each plan with dissociated imagery. Watch yourself in your picture, go through your actions that deal with the worry. If you feel good about that plan, then mentally rehearse it in an associated way. Step into the picture and imagine yourself actually going through those actions. Notice how you feel. You will feel more resourceful and in control. Go through the sequence for each worry:

Mentally rehearse (dissociated) – watch yourself acting your plan.

↓

If not satisfied, think of another plan and question how far this really is under your control.

↓

When you are satisfied, step into the picture and mentally rehearse the action (associated).

↓

Feel good.

↓

Move on!

Figure 6.4: Mental rehearsal

Worry and anxiety come from the future, but emotions about the past can also disturb your concentration. For example, you may face a very similar situation to one in the past which you bungled badly. Or you may face an opponent who thrashed you the last time you played them. You may have to take a goal kick when you missed the last one you took. These sorts of experiences can dent your confidence. In the next chapter I will describe a process that will take the hurt out of these experiences so they will not affect you any more.

Some athletes feel guilty about letting themselves down, or the team down, or their coach or parents. All these unpleasant emotions come from the past. When you are living in the present moment, you cannot feel anxious because the future is yet to come – you are creating it by what you are doing now. The past has gone, it has simply led up to what is happening now. Now there is no room for distracting emotions, there is just present moment awareness.

The Present Moment

Being in the present is the answer to many sports problems and it is the key to top sports performance. When you stay in the present moment, you cannot be distracted by emotions like guilt or anxiety and you play every point and part of the game on its merit. The present moment is the only place where you can enter the zone.

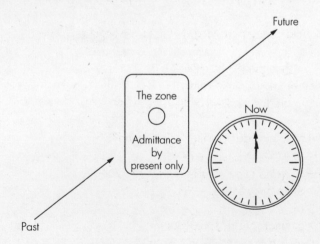

Figure 6.5: The present moment

How ironic that the answer to peak performance is to be where you are anyway! Peak performance is not some unattainable Everest but as close as your next game. All you have to do is stop making it difficult for yourself.

The best way to connect with the present moment is through your body. The old maxim of 'Know yourself' being the key to wisdom applies to athletes in a relevant way – know your physical body. Be sensitive to it and aware of the messages that it gives you. It is worth investing a few minutes of your time every day just to relax and tune into your body. It is especially good after you finish your mental rehearsal practice routines to relax and clear your mind before returning to your everyday tasks.

You can use the following exercise at any time.

Exercise 32: Awareness

Sit quietly for a few moments and become aware of your body.

> What are you aware of?
> What feelings do you have in your body?
> Start at your feet and let your awareness move up your body.
> Feel the connection between all the parts of the body.
> Which parts feel at ease and which parts feel uncomfortable?

Do not try to change anything, just notice, without judging.

> What thoughts do you have?
> Look at any mental pictures.
> What are the qualities of these pictures?

> What sounds do you hear in your mind?
> Are you talking to yourself?
> What sort of voice quality does this have?
> Are there any other sounds?

> What emotional state are you in?
> What is your predominant emotion?

Be aware of it without trying to change anything.

> How is your sense of balance?
> Do you feel like you are leaning too far to one side, or too far
> backward or forwards?

Come back to the present moment.

When you do this exercise just be aware of your thoughts without judging them. Notice how they come and go, ebb and flow of their own
accord. You do not have to make any effort to think, it happens by itself.
Your unconscious generates a whole current of thoughts that seem to
rise up out of nowhere like a stream welling out of the ground. You
can't plug the spring, so just watch and bathe in the flow. When you
watch, you realize that you are not your thoughts, you are more than
your thoughts. You do not have to jump and satisfy every thought that
pulls for your attention. You can be quiet and still and watch and listen
in the present moment. When you do that, you are in a place very close
to the zone, that empty state of mind where everything flows.

Emotional Balance

Emotional balance and energy levels are important in a match and they
are also part of the wider balance in your life. Sport is part of life, a
good part, a satisfying part, but still only a part. Sport usually means
physical activity and that brings out the neurochemicals, the endorphins
that make you feel good, so you get a 'high' from sport and exercise. It's
a natural high, it's legal and it's free. But it can have a price.

One price is overtraining. When you overtrain or over-exercise,
instead of feeling energized, you will feel tired. Over-exercise depresses
the immune system and you may suffer more illness than usual. Too
much exercise will make you feel lethargic and heavy, just like too little
exercise.

Too much mental rehearsal will not help either. Don't try to do
everything all at once. Pick a few exercises in this book and try them.
Test them out. Only use what works for you and you feel congruent
about. If a technique or exercise does not work after you have given it
a fair trial, then drop it and try something else. There are many possible

approaches in this book and only you will know the right one for you –
it will be what works.

Do you want to win?

I hope so.

Do you want to be the best you can be?

I hope so.

But . . . at all costs?

There is a saying that you can have whatever you want if you are
willing to pay the price, but you may find the prize you win is not
worth the price you paid. Some athletes take drugs to help them build
muscle to gain a slight advantage to win. Winning means money,
praise and admiration. But they always have a sneaking suspicion that
it's the drug that achieved the triumph. No one likes to feel that the
name of a steroid drug should be engraved on the cup, or a bottle of
chemicals should really occupy the winner's podium.

The practice and commitment of athletes are incredible. The top
athletes deserve their success, but sometimes even they pay a price of
repeated injuries. Some athletes break down continually and retire early
or have a series of operations because they put their body under too
much stress. I don't think this is what success is about. In a similar way
some athletes will mask injuries and pain with drugs. This may work
once or twice but if they do it repeatedly then they risk severely injur-
ing themselves and having to stay out of sport for months instead of
weeks – and nearly all drugs have side-effects. Pain is your body's way
of saying '*Stop!* There's something wrong.' It's a signal that needs
attention, however uncomfortable it might be and however much you
would like to ignore it.

Sporting triumph is wonderful but short-lived. Champions have to
live with the price after the cheering has died away and younger, faster,
stronger athletes have replaced them. Sport enriches your life, but you
need to have a satisfying life outside sport to enrich.

My younger daughter showed a talent for gymnastics at an early
age and was picked to join an élite squad of young gymnasts at her
local club. She enjoyed it very much and got on well with her friends in
the squad. They did exhibitions and examinations. All the girls were
under nine. After two years what began as a pleasure became a chore.
The magic had gone. She would go to school during the day then train
five evenings a week for three hours and come home exhausted. She
found it difficult to keep up with her schoolwork and her social life

suffered. She got on well with her friends in the squad, but she started to find that they were the only friends she had time for. Some of the gymnastics moves involved being able to dislocate parts of the body at will. Good gymnasts have to be able to dislocate their shoulder blades to do some moves. My daughter suffered a series of niggling injuries. There were days when she was in constant pain. Finally she gave up gymnastics. The price was greater than we were willing to pay.

Many athletes are prepared to pay a big price for success. No one can say they are right or wrong. Just be aware *for yourself* of the price you are paying and whether you will be happy to have paid it when you look back in a few years' time.

CHAPTER SIX SUMMARY

Emotions give energy and intensity that can work for you or against you:

Too little intensity can lead to low energy, poor motivation and defeatism and can make you easily distracted.
Too much intensity can lead to tense muscles, anxiety, too narrow a focus of concentration and emotional outbursts.

You need the right balance of emotional energy to play at your best.
  You get the right balance from the balance of challenge and resources.
  When perceived challenge is greater than your perceived resources, then you are in the panic zone — too much emotional intensity.
  When you do not think you are challenged sufficiently, then you can feel in the drone zone — too little emotional intensity.
  You may move between panic, balance and drone all in the same match.

When you lack emotional intensity you can:

- Use an anchor to get more energy.
- Shout or use rhythmic chanting.
- Associate into your body and into the present moment.
- Focus on your body.
- Act *as if* you have more energy. When you want to feel something, act as if you already have it.

When you need less emotional intensity:

- Use relaxing imagery.
- Broaden your focus of attention, using peripheral vision.
- Turn your attention outwards. Look at the scene, listen to the sounds in the environment.
- Dissociate to regain control.

■ Centre yourself in the present moment.

Breathing is a powerful way of changing your physiology and
energy level.
> Anxiety and excitement have a very similar physiology and
> set of feelings, except the breathing pattern is different.
> You can calm yourself by rhythmic breathing – take twice as
> long to breathe out as you do to breathe in.

Anxiety before the game can stop you playing at your best.
> Performance anxiety usually consists of:

■ associated pictures of failure or ridicule
■ self-talk about all the things that could go wrong
■ unpleasant feelings about the pictures and self-talk

Sometimes we are not aware of this process.
> Performance anxiety is all thought and no action. You worry
> about things over which you have no control. It is all
> based on imaginary events that have not happened.

To deal with performance anxiety:

■ Relax and be aware of your feelings.
■ Explore your pictures and internal dialogue.
■ Be clear what is under your control and what is out of your control.
■ Make a plan for each worry that is under your control.
■ Mentally rehearse the plan (dissociated).

When you are satisfied, mentally rehearse the plan with associated imagery.

Keep a balance between the demands of your sport and the
rest of your life.

After the Game

Learning from your Performance

You have played your match, competed in your event. Win, lose or draw, good or bad, it's over. The spectators have gone home. You have celebrated with your friends and teammates, talked over what happened with your coach. You may feel elated or depressed. Sometimes drawing or even losing an excellent hard-fought match can be more satisfying than winning a match where you played badly, but your opponent played worse. Whatever the result, it is now in the score book. Numbers on a page, devoid of emotion, give no clue to the sweat, energy and feeling that went into the game. Those were your experience and now they are the memory that you take home with you. Whatever happened, you have done your best. Now you can learn from what happened to two ways.

No one is the perfect sporting machine, so you will have made mistakes and you will want to make sure that you do not repeat them. Mistakes happen, no one is perfect, even the greatest players have their good days and bad days, but you don't want to make the same mistake twice. Mistakes are feedback to help you become an even better player in future. They may be painful and infuriating at the time, but dealing with them is the way to improve. Look on your mistakes as a coach would – they tell you what you have to change in order to play better. A repeated mistake is a nagging coach.

Secondly, learn from your successes. No competent coach would correct your mistakes without praising your good play as well. We often take good play for granted and only notice mistakes, but studying your good play will allow you to understand it better. You can analyse the thoughts, feelings, beliefs, values and skills that went into that time and so have a better chance of playing like that next time. NLP calls this 'self-modelling'. Good performance is not random, dependent on the weather or what you had for breakfast. Remember when you played your very best. You have that skill within you. If you can do it once,

you can do it again. You can make what was your best performance
your normal level of performance.

The next exercise will help you learn from your mistakes and turn
them into insight. It is an excellent exercise to use after every major
game, especially if you played badly or made a lot of mistakes.

Exercise 33: Mistakes to Insight

Part 1: Review

Find some time when you can relax later in the same day as your game.
Wait until you get home and you have ten minutes when you will not be
disturbed. Don't try to do this exercise immediately.

1   Imagine a friend had followed you around with a video camera
    and had taped everything that happened. It was an unusual
    videotape because you could view it from any angle and zoom
    in and out at will using your remote control.
    Relax and prepare to watch the video.
    See yourself at the beginning of the event. Do not associate into the
    picture – yet! Watch it as you might watch *Match of the Day* on
    television.

2   See yourself playing. Be your own coach. Make mental notes
    about what you did, what was good, what could be improved.
    Notice any mistakes or poor play. Stay out of the picture,
    concentrate on that athlete on video who looks and sounds so
    like you. What could you do to help them?
    If you find yourself wincing or feeling bad when you see the
    mistakes, then you have partly associated into the picture. Step out
    and watch it dispassionately.
    One reason we do not learn from our mistakes is it is not pleasant
    to review them. Once was enough! Why go over them? Once is
    enough to *do* them, but after that it depends *how* you go over
    them. If you were to review them associated you would be back
    there, doing them again. This would not only feel bad, but would
    mentally rehearse them for the future. When you view them
    dissociated, you can learn from them because you are not
    involved, so they are impersonal and interesting.

3 Once you have watched the video through, think about what you saw.

Where could your play be improved?
What are the weaknesses?
What do you need to do to make sure that the mistakes do not happen again?
What can you learn from that tape?
Were there any errors that were really bad and might affect your confidence in the future?
Were there any toe-curling mistakes that might keep you awake at night and would earn you an earful from your coach? If there are, you need to deal with them now so that they do not come back to haunt you or sap your future confidence.

Part 2: Dealing with Disasters

1 View the major errors again. Stay dissociated and check that you feel resourceful while you view them. View them from just before the error, when the game was fine, to just afterwards when the mistake was made and you were back to playing normally again.
2 Now imagine the scene running *backwards*. Imagine playing the same film clip of the error, but run it backward from after it had happened to before it was going to happen. Imagine you are pressing the rewind button on the video.
3 When you have done that switch off. Flip the tape to after the error (*without seeing the error*) then run it backwards again even faster.
4 Do this at least three times, each time getting faster. How does that change your view of that error? You should have a completely different perspective.
5 Try to think about the error in the same way now. If you still feel bad about it, associate into the picture after the mistake and imagine it backwards – the same process as just described, but now you are associated into the videotape. This is the mental equivalent of 'undoing' the error.

This process garbles the memory. You won't think about the error in the same way again and the memory won't come back to haunt you like a family ghost.

Part 3: What Do You Want Instead?

Now think what you want to happen instead.

> Where exactly do you need to play better?
> What mistakes do you want to change?
> What were you trying to achieve in those situations?

Whatever it was, see yourself achieving it. Create a new video of how you would have liked the game to go. Don't change what your opponents do, change *your* play. Stay dissociated, but see yourself playing exactly how you want. See everything going well, with no mistakes. You are making the perfect video of the match, worthy of being on *Match of the Day*. You play beautifully. All mistakes are edited out and replaced by excellent play.

When you are completely satisfied with this new tape, associate into it and *live it as if it were happening now*. Imagine you are there actually playing, see through your own eyes, be completely associated and star in your own production. Feel good about playing the way you want to.

This exercise does not deny the result; it's not wishful thinking. What happened has happened, the result is in the score book and can't be changed. What you are changing is *how you think about it*. You can't change the past, but you can change how you think about the past to make sure you do not have to relive it again. You are turning what could have been a liability into a resource. Now you could label that video with the date, give it a title and put it in your personal video store, filed safely in your mind.

Exercise 34: Enjoying your Sport – Your 'Greatest Hits'

You can do this exercise together with the last one or on its own.

Look at your mental video of a recent game or event, only this time see the times when you played really well. Stay dissociated and watch yourself. Pay attention to where you excelled and where you were really enjoying yourself. Pick two or three of the best instances.

Now associate only into those parts. Feel what they were like again. See what you saw then and hear what you heard. Recapture those feelings and enjoy the moments.

When you have finished, imagine editing that tape and snipping out the best bits. Imagine transferring them to another videotape where you store all your greatest moments. This is your 'Greatest Hits' video.

Store this mental video away. Whenever you feel stale or lack confidence, pull it out and view it. This is how you can play.

You will never lose those times and they will provide good material for your resourceful anchors. When you go through the unconscious review of resources exercise (*Exercise 23, see page 109*) this imaginary videotape will make it easier.

Dealing with Injury

You may have the bad luck to be injured in your sport. Being aware of your body and controlling your intensity will make injury less likely, but accidents still happen. Most injuries are minor, but they are annoying enough to stop you playing for days or weeks. Severe injury will put you out for months. Even very slight injuries can make it difficult to play – either they are painful or they hold you back because you don't trust yourself. Some injuries will not even have anything to do with sport yet they could stop you playing. I remember bruising my toe one day and not giving it another thought. I was due to play squash that night, but it didn't worry me – I don't play squash with my toe! But that night I was surprised how much trouble it was and how it stopped me playing well. The constant movement of stopping and starting kept jarring it and making it painful. Another time I had hurt my right thumb and this made it hard to hold the racquet. It seemed so unfair that a slight injury could effectively stop me playing.

You may hurt yourself while you are playing, but the thrill of the game, coupled with the endorphins careering around your bloodstream, may tempt you to play on through the pain. Yet pain is the body's signal to stop so you don't hurt yourself even more. Pay attention to it.

When you know your body, you will be able to tell whether the injury is serious and whether you should stop immediately. Sometimes a serious injury may not actually hurt very much at the time. A few years ago I was playing and suddenly found I could not bend at the waist to pick up the ball. My back seemed to have locked. It didn't hurt and I had no warning, no previous twinge when I might have twisted it. I could have played on (as long as I didn't try and bend down). I decided not to, even though I was not in pain, because back injuries can be serious. I had a horrible feeling that the pain would come the next morning and I did not want to compound it. Part of me wanted to play on, but you need to get down to the ball in squash, so I would not have played very well anyway. Sure enough, I was very stiff the next morning, but osteopathy and some healing visualization got me back on court within two weeks. I still have no idea what caused it.

When we hurt ourselves, the pain is usually caused by inflammation, which is the first stage of the healing process. Inflammation helps increase the blood flow to the injury, so the neurochemicals that are needed can do their healing work in the long term. In the short term, inflammation can be very painful.

What can a mental approach contribute to healing? Injuries are real and physical. There is, however, also a mental aspect. How you think about an injury can affect how well it heals. We know from the study of placebos that patients who are given treatments that have no proven *medical* effect can recover well because these treatments mobilize the patient's *belief* in recovery. Healing involves both mental and physical factors.

None of the healing suggestions here are substitutes for medical treatment. Severe trauma like broken bones or torn ligaments needs immediate hospital treatment. Many injuries will need physiotherapy or osteopathy. The suggestions in this book are meant to complement medical treatments and physical procedures, not replace them.

There are many mental approaches that can help healing. First you need to deal with the actual trauma. You didn't mean to injure yourself; you can run the previous 'Mistakes to Insight' process *(Exercise 33)* on the injury as if it were a mistake.

The mind holds an injury as well as the body. Unless you change your thinking about it, your mind may turn it over repeatedly, sometimes when you are not even aware of it. This can act as a form of associated mental rehearsal – you are actually deepening the pathway of thoughts and actions that led up to the injury. When you change the way you think about the injury, you will also change the way your body responds to it.

Even after the injury heals you may feel hesitant 'just in case'. I know many athletes, particularly tennis players, who have started to play again after an injury, but don't seem to believe that they are completely healed. They are more hesitant, they hold back on their shots and, as any coach will tell you, one way to get injured is to hold back, because that creates a counter tension in the muscles, pulling them two ways at once. This makes injury more likely, not less.

I believe you can speed up your healing process by using imagery and I speak from personal experience. A few years ago I suffered from tennis elbow. The elbow is a delicate place. All the joints of the body are more prone to injury because they have to move and be flexible, but there is always a danger of too much movement, or movement in the wrong direction. All the tendons and nerves that work the hand and fingers attach to the muscle sheath just below the elbow. If they are subjected to repetitive strain or extreme tension, that part becomes inflamed – this is so-called 'tennis elbow'. The pain is in the elbow, but the cause is usually in the wrist. If the inflammation is bad, then pinching anything between your fingers and thumb is painful and cleaning your teeth becomes torture. You don't have to play tennis to get tennis elbow – any repetitive twisting and gripping movement can cause it. My sin was over-enthusiastic DIY work. I then played squash several times while my elbow was slightly inflamed and this made it much worse. As soon as I knew what was happening, I took great care because tennis elbow can become chronic, never completely healing. Tennis elbow generally heals slowly, because healing needs a good blood supply and the elbow, being literally out on a limb, without major vessels going through it, has a very poor blood supply. Physiotherapy and osteopathy both helped, and I used the accelerated healing process in the next exercise. My elbow healed very well and I played as well as ever when I resumed.

My elbow taught me a number of valuable lessons. First, I learned to pay attention to my body and not to aggravate an injury. I also learned that the weakest, most vulnerable point is usually the one that gets injured. My elbow seemed like the culprit, but it was innocent, I had put too much pressure on it. My elbow was under strain because I have very mobile bones in my wrist, they can turn far more than most, so I can twist the tendons more than normal. I also broke my right wrist (I am right handed) when I was 14 and it set a little bit twisted. So when I was putting up the wardrobe and playing squash, I was twisting the tendons more than they could bear, and all the force was concentrated in the small area where they insert into the muscle just below the elbow. You play sport with your whole body and because we use a lot of force, any small imbalance can have effects elsewhere.

When my daughter was doing gymnastics, her right Achilles tendon became very painful. The Achilles tendon is the thick band that connects the back of the heel to the leg muscle. It has to work whenever you move your foot. It is called the Achilles tendon after the legend of Achilles, the hero of Greek myth. The legend goes that when he was a baby, his mother plunged him into the murky waters of the Styx, river of the underworld. All that was immersed in the water became invulnerable to hurt. But Achilles' mother had to hold him somewhere or he would have been swept away, so she held him by the heel. So, his heel was the only place he could be hurt and as nobody thought to hurt him there, he seemed unbeatable until the Trojan warrior Paris learned his secret and killed him by striking at his heel.

The Achilles tendon is very strong and absolutely crucial to any movement of the foot. My daughter rested from gymnastics for a few weeks and had physiotherapy on her foot and leg, but when she started again, the pain came back. She also started to have pain down the front of her thigh on the other leg. Physiotherapy had little effect on that. We were at a loss, until a Chinese osteopath found the cause. My daughter had twisted her hip in a gymnastics exercise and it was slightly misaligned. To compensate, she had shifted her weight and that had put more strain on the Achilles tendon. She then walked slightly differently and because she was not balanced, this put extra weight on the other thigh. Once the osteopath had realigned her hip (with an audible crack!), her thigh and Achilles tendon returned to normal, and she was able to take up gymnastics again after a couple of weeks' rest. The body is a wonderfully balanced mechanism and pain may show up in a quite different place from the problem that causes it.

Exercise 35: Accelerated Healing

Part 1: Dealing with the Trauma

1   You can use this process on any injury, not just a sports injury. The first step is to deal with the trauma of the injury with a process like that described in Exercise 33, page 160. Play your mental video of when the injury happened. Make sure you are dissociated. Watch the video from just before you were injured to just after the injury when you had stopped playing. Imagine you are coaching that athlete that looks and sounds like you.

How would you advise that athlete?
What do they need to do differently next time so that they do not injure themselves again?
What can you learn from the incident that can help you in the future?
What were they trying to achieve when they injured themselves?
How could they have achieved that without injury?

2   Stop the tape at a suitable point after the injury has occurred, at a time when you are comfortable and no longer playing. Associate into the image. Run the tape backwards while you are associated in the image. Imagine being in the situation again, but living it backwards. You start injured, then suddenly you are not injured and you have run time backwards in your mind. Then blank the tape.

3   Now dissociate and run the tape forward. *Do not associate here!* If you do, you will be rehearsing the injury. Repeat the process – associate into the image and run it backwards faster. Then dissociate and repeat the process at least three times.

4   What were you trying to do when you hurt yourself? What goals were you trying to achieve? See yourself in a movie doing that without hurting yourself. Make the move differently or do nothing. If you were injured accidentally by your opponent, see yourself

anticipating the situation and moving out of the way in good time.

When you are satisfied, associate into the new video and rehearse that at least three times to erase the mental imprint of the injury. That does not mean that your injury will be miraculously gone, of course, but when the mind does not hang on to the memory, it is easier for the body to let it go as well. The body's memory is the actual hurt. When the body 'forgets' the hurt, it has healed.

Part 2: The Healing Process

Your body heals itself all the time. You constantly get cuts and bruises and you don't have to do anything directly, they heal by themselves. Healing is an unconscious process that works perfectly nearly every time. Your body carries a blueprint of health and wholeness. Inflammation and even pain are part of the healing process. You can model this natural healing process and use imagery to help it take place even more smoothly. This is a variation of the process first published by Steve and Connirae Andreas in their book *Heart of the Mind*.

1   Focus on the injury you have. Find out as much as possible about it from books, the Internet and talking to people. When I had tennis elbow, I became an authority on it, so much so that I think I might have bored any of my friends who were unwise enough to ask how I was. You need to know how the injured part of the body works so that you can do clear imagery on it.

2   How will you know the injury has healed? What will you be able to do when the injury is healed that you do not do now? My answer was to play squash again and your answer may be to play your sport again, but it need not be this.

3   Think of a past injury that was similar to your injury now and healed successfully. It does not have to be sport related and it does not have to be exactly the same. Let your mind wander and a perfect example will occur to you. I used an example of when I twisted my knee five years before.

4   You healed this injury. Think back to what it was like as it was healing. How do you think about it? Imagine the healing process. What image do you have? Look at the submodalities. What are you seeing?

Is there a colour?
Is it a moving image?
Whereabouts do you see it?
How far away is it?
Are you associated or dissociated in the image?
Are there any other significant aspects to the image?

Listen and notice if there are any auditory submodalities.
Do you hear anything?
Are you talking to yourself?
What are you saying and what tone of voice are you using?
Whereabouts do the sounds come from?
Are there any other significant qualities of the sound?

What are the feelings associated with the healing?
How large an area do they cover?
Are they warm or cold?
Do they feel rough or smooth?
Are there any other qualities to the feelings that seem important?

Make a list of the submodality qualities *(see example below)*.
These submodalities are important. *They are how your mind thinks
about healing.* Whenever you want to heal yourself, this is the way
you need to think about the injury.

5   Now do the same submodality analysis of your present injury.
List those submodalities beside the ones of the healing process.
What are the significant differences?
There may be very few or no differences, in which case the injury
is healing naturally and easily, like the previous one. However,
sometimes injuries seem to take longer to heal, or become
chronic, in which case you will find some differences in the two
submodality structures.

ACCELERATING HEALING – EXAMPLE

Submodalities of Healing

Present injury	Past injury that has healed very well
Visual submodalities	*Visual submodalities*
dissociated – I see myself with the injury	associated – I am looking at my knee
black and white picture	fleshy colour
little movement	sense of pulsing movement
Auditory submodalities	*Auditory submodalities*
no sounds	no sounds
Kinesthetic submodalities	*Kinesthetic submodalities*
cool feeling around the injury	warm feeling

6 Map over the submodalities of the good healing experience to the present injury. In the above example, I would think of the present injury as an associated picture, I would give the picture colour and movement, and then give it pulsating warmth. Concentrate on this image for a few minutes twice a day.

7 Treat the part of your body that is injured like a good friend. Don't get angry or impatient with it because it won't do your bidding. Do not get annoyed when it hurts you. Forgive it. This may sound odd, but when you think about it, you may find that you are angry with that part of your body, that you are somehow blaming it for being hurt. Those feelings don't help you.

8 Make sure you think about your injury in a wider sense than just getting back to playing. When I was injured, I enjoyed my time resting. If you keep thinking how much longer it will be before you can play again, it will seem more frustrating and the time will seem to go more slowly – the more aware of time you are, the more slowly it seems to go. Make sure you learn from the injury and

change your game so that you do not make the same mistake again. If you just heal the injury and go back to playing as you did before, the odds are you will injure yourself in exactly the same way as you did before.

Remember that when you are injured, you may not be able to play your sport, but you can still mentally rehearse and use imagery to improve.

The Last Lap

Sport plays an important part in your life – you are taking it seriously enough to read this book and work with these exercises. If you use them consistently, they will transform your game. I am sure you will have seen that many of them can be used in other situations in your life, they need not be confined to sport. Sport is a reflection of the rest of your life.

What part does sport play in your life? You decide how much effort you put into it and what you want to get out of it. One joy of sport is the competition. You strive against your competitors and you strive against yourself. Whenever you play, you are playing against your own limitations, striving to be better, to get more satisfaction. There is pleasure in the sheer joy of movement, joy in competing, in developing your skills, win or lose. You feel the glow as the endorphins work their magic on your nerve endings and you feel the warmth of your friendships with fellow athletes. Sport is a wonderful and rewarding part of life whatever your standard. Keep pushing your limits whether you are at the Olympic Games or the local football club. Grab those moments and enjoy them. I overheard a locker-room conversation one evening while I was finishing this book. Two men in their mid forties were talking about a younger player.

'Typical youth,' one said. 'Thinks he knows it all and doesn't listen.'

'He's damn good,' said the other. 'But he doesn't work, he just coasts along, thinks he can go like that forever.'

'Yeah, I wish I had half his talent, but I can still hold my own with him, sometimes he gives up.'

'Maybe he'll realize one day. When your knees start to rock and roll and you don't see the ball like you used to, that's when you wish you had worked when you could. I wish I could tell him. No regrets.'

Imagine yourself in a few years time and imagine looking back on what you are doing now. Would you say you are getting the most from your life and your sport? Are you taking the moments right now and really enjoying each one? When you play sport you have a chance to move, compete, win and enjoy. Sport is like the rest of your life, only more so.

Here's a final exercise to review your talents.

Exercise 36: Review

Do this exercise when you are relaxed and have about ten minutes when you will not be disturbed.

1 Imagine the place where you play. Imagine looking around. See the typical field or court and imagine your opponents as well. Feel the sun in your face and the wind in your hair if your sport is one played outside. Recreate that typical playing environment.

2 Imagine yourself playing well.

What skills do you have?
What strengths do you have?
What aspects of the game are you really good at?
Think of all your technical skills in your sport and also all the mental skills that reinforce those.

3 Imagine yourself playing 'in the zone', totally concentrated, in the present moment. Time goes slowly, but you go fast.

4 What is important to you about your sport?
Why do you play it?
What do you value about it?
What do you particularly enjoy about it?
Think of all the positive consequences, fitness, the joy of movement, friends, your social life and all the times you have won and achieved your goals.

5 Now think of yourself as an athlete. Who are you? What sort of athlete are you?
Think of some symbol, some metaphor for yourself as an athlete.
Many athletes think of an animal, an animal that has grace and

fluidity of movement as well as enormous strength. Swimmers often think of themselves as dolphins. Sometimes these metaphors get attached as nicknames to athletes, for example Tiger Woods and Greg Norman, the great white shark. Your metaphor does not have to be an animal. It could be a symbol, a sound, a feeling, an action or a film clip. Take whatever comes into your mind that seems to express your essential identity as an athlete.

6 How does your identity of an athlete fit into your whole life? What part does it play? If life is a game, what part do you have in it? Again, a metaphor is the most appropriate way to express this; words are not adequate to completely express these sorts of relationships. Think of your family and friends, loved ones and acquaintances. How do you, the athlete, relate to them? How does your metaphor for your identity as an athlete enrich your wider web of social relationships?

7 Take this enrichment and think about your identity as an athlete. How does that wider view illuminate who you are and your metaphor?

8 Take that metaphor of identity and bring it into what you value about sport. Think again about what is important to you about sport and what you value about it. Notice how that becomes wider and more fulfilling when it is linked with your identity as an athlete and how that identity relates to the rest of your life and relationships.

9 Take the sense of what is important to you now about sport and bring it into your skills. Imagine how well you could play and how satisfying it could be if you had that feeling, that connection and that metaphor in the back of your mind whenever you went out to play.

10 Finally, come back to where you are now. All those skills, those values, those thoughts and feelings are yours. You have them wherever you are.

Play well and enjoy the game.

REFERENCES

Steve and Connirae Andreas, *Heart of the Mind*, Real People Press, 1989

CHAPTER SEVEN SUMMARY

After a game, review your performance:

- to learn from your mistakes so they do not happen again
- to model your moments of excellence so you can have them more often and more consistently

Learn from your mistakes by watching them again using dissociated imagery.
  Scramble the memory by seeing it backwards.
  Decide what you want to do instead and mentally rehearse that using associated imagery.

Go back over your best play, analyse it and enjoy it again.
  Remember it as a resource for unconscious processing of your best play.

Use imagery to help heal any injury.
  Mental approaches to healing do not replace, but complement and enhance normal medical treatment.
  Treat any injury as if it were a mistake. Use imagery to see it again dissociated and learn from it. Scramble the memory by seeing it backwards.
  Then mentally rehearse, associated, what you wanted to happen without getting injured.
  Injuries happen to the weakest point in the body that takes the strain.
  The cause of the pain may not be in the same place as the pain.
  Think about your injury using the critical submodalities of your normal healing process to speed the healing.

Enjoy your sport as part of a greater game.

Appendix I

Fitness and Exercise

Any fitness and exercise programme must start from your present level of fitness. Fitness comes from exercise. You can use this next questionnaire to evaluate your present level of exercise. A good exercise programme is built by balancing the following:

- the frequency of exercise – how often
- the duration of exercise – how long
- the intensity of exercise – how much effort

First give yourself a score on how frequently you exercise.

Frequency	Score
Six times a week	10
Five times a week	9
Four times a week	8
Three times a week	7
Twice a week	6
Once a week	5
Once a fortnight	4
Once a month	3
Occasionally	2
Never	1
Score	_____

Next, give yourself a duration score: how long are your exercise sessions?

Duration	Score
Over 30 minutes	5
20–30 minutes	4
15–20 minutes	3
10–15 minutes	2
Under 10 minutes	1
Score	_____

Finally give yourself an intensity score: how much effort do you put in?

Intensity	Score
Heavy (sustained heavy breathing during the exercise)	6
Heavy but not sustained (for example in squash or tennis)	5
Moderate but sustained (for example in running or cycling)	4
Moderate intermittent	3
Light	2
Hardly raise a sweat	1
Score	_____

Take these three scores and multiply them together.
Your basic fitness score (BFS) = frequency (F) times duration (D) times intensity (I):

BFS = F x D x I

Basic Fitness Score

Over 240	You are probably over-exercising. Cut down.
180 to 240	An excellent score, you have a very active lifestyle.
180 to 160	A good score that shows an active lifestyle. This is the level you need to get the full health benefits of exercise
160 to 130	A healthy lifestyle and moderate fitness.
130 to 100	Acceptable, but could do better. Either exercise more frequently or for longer to get the health and fitness benefits.
100 to 60	Insufficient to maintain fitness or give the health benefits of exercise.
Under 60	Are you asleep? Start moving!

THE FOUR TYPES OF FITNESS

Who would you say was the fittest athlete:

- a champion weightlifter?
- a long distance runner?
- a gymnast?
- a 100-metre sprinter?
- a footballer?

Of course they are all fit, but in different ways. There is no absolute standard of fitness that can be applied across all sports. The type of fitness you need depends on the sport you engage in.

There are four types of fitness, known as the 'Four S Formula':

Speed
Strength
Stamina
Suppleness

Design your exercise programme to develop those that are most needed in your sport.

- *Speed* is the time it takes to complete a movement. It may be a quick delicate movement as in badminton or a sustained run down the field in rugby or soccer.
- *Strength* is the maximum force that you can exert in one muscle contraction.

  Most of us possess far more strength than we think, but it needs an emergency to show itself. There are many stories of people who performed what for them were superhuman tasks because they were caught up in an extraordinary situation. One dramatic example of hidden strength is that of an Australian woman who was outside working on her car when it fell off the jack, pinning her 11-year-old son underneath. The woman weighed only 123 lb, but she was alone and believed her son would die crushed under the car within a few minutes. She picked up the car with her bare hands and held it up for long enough for her son to crawl out. The car weighed one and a half tonnes and she cracked three vertebrae because her spine compressed so much. Muscle is stronger than bone and will and imagination can be stronger than both.
- *Stamina* is the ability to maintain speed and/or strength over long periods. We all begin the game fresh, but our speed and strength decline the longer we play.
- *Suppleness* comes from stretching muscles groups. Every sport extends some muscles more than others and the more supple you are, the less your risk of injury through torn ligaments or twisted joints. The sport where you need the most suppleness is gymnastics.

Speed, strength, suppleness and stamina are mental as well as physical qualities. We talk about 'speed of thought', 'strength of mind' and 'mental flexibility'. Determination and stubbornness are the mental equivalents of stamina. Also when we 'put our mind' to it, we can often go beyond our perceived physical limitations. There are many examples like the Australian lady lifting the car that suggest we all have much more strength than we normally use. You may have had a similar experience when you were able to go beyond what you thought you were capable of.

Does speed have a mental aspect? Of course. Our body only reacts as fast as our mind pays attention. So our physical speed depends on our mental alertness. When you are preoccupied with your own thoughts you do not react so quickly. By focusing and dealing with distractions you can increase your speed.

The more motivated you are, the more energy you bring to your play and the more strength, stamina and speed you can achieve. Physical training can take you to your limits – in ordinary circumstances. Your mind can take you beyond those limits.

Suppleness has a mental aspect too. Try this experiment.

Stand up and make sure you have room to stretch and swing your arms. Hold your right arm straight out in front of you at shoulder height and point forward with your index finger. Look along the line of your finger into the distance.

Now swing your arm around backwards as far as it will comfortably go, until you are pointing behind you. Continue to look along your arm to your finger and notice what you are pointing at. Then drop your arm and look forward again.

Stay still and *imagine* pointing your arm again to the front. Imagine swinging it backwards easily and effortlessly as far as it can go. Imagine your shoulder supple and relaxed so you can swing it further than you did before. Imagine looking down your arm and seeing how much further round you can see.

Now do a real test. Pick up your arm (in a manner of speaking) and extend it in front of you again. Point forwards and then, without thinking of anything in particular, swing it back behind you as far as you comfortably can. Look along your arm to where you are pointing. Are you pointing further than before?

Most people find they are pointing further. For some, it is a lot further. A few moments thought has had a big physical effect.

Now do the same exercise with your other arm, so both sides of your body get the benefit of being more supple.

Will and imagination can amplify your basic fitness beyond what you believed possible.

AEROBIC FITNESS

Aerobic or cardiovascular fitness is the ability to take in, transport and utilize oxygen. It improves lung capacity and allows the heart and cardiovascular system to work more efficiently. It is achieved by aerobic exercise that brings your heart rate into the training zone – between 70 and 80 per cent of your maximum heart rate. Your maximum heart rate declines with age and is defined in beats per minute. It is 220 minus your age beats per minute.

Maximum heart rate = (220 – your age) beats per minute.

For example, aerobic exercise for a 40-year-old athlete would bring their heart rate to between 136 and 144 beats per minute (between 70 and 80 per cent of 180).

Aerobic exercise, undertaken three to five times a week, is the road to basic fitness. It will increase your speed and stamina.

The most important part of aerobic training is getting the heart rate into the training zone and keeping it there for the duration of the exercise. To set up an aerobic training programme start at what is comfortable and gradually increase the frequency, duration or intensity, depending on the demands of your sport. For example if you are a runner you could run the same distance at a faster pace (to increase speed), run further at the same pace (to increase endurance), or gradually increase the pace and the distance together (to increase stamina). Endurance is achieved by repeated muscle contractions and is probably the most important component of fitness in most sports. Training is always specific. Train the muscles you use the most in your sport.

To build your fitness, you need aerobic exercise over and above basic exercise to maintain good health. There are many books that will help you *(see Bibliography)* and there are also many health and fitness clubs that offer advice. Consult a doctor before embarking on any new or unfamiliar exercise regime.

EXERCISE GUIDELINES

Here are few general guidelines for any fitness training:

1 *Personalize your training according to the results you want to achieve.* The higher your level of competition, the more demanding your training regime needs to be. Remember you get the results you train for, so train the right muscles. Think about your sport in terms of

the four components of fitness – strength, stamina, speed and suppleness. What does it need?

Draw a diagram to show the relative importance of each for your sport.

For example, my sport is squash. For that, stamina is the most important of the four components, while speed and suppleness are important too. Strength is less important.

Figure 8.1: Fitness for squash

I arrange my training so I spend half my training time on stamina, a quarter of my time on speed, a little less on suppleness and I build strength only where I need it.

2 *Always warm up and cool down.* Warming up prepares the body to work. A good warm up increases the body temperature, respiration and heart rate. It also pre-stretches the muscles and ligaments so you are less likely to injure yourself. A good warm up is important in its own right, not something to get out of the way as quickly as possible to get on with the 'real' business of exercise. Your warm up should also include some stretching exercises.

The cool down is important too. If you suddenly stop vigorous exercise your blood circulation quickly becomes sluggish, the blood pools and the waste products produced by the exercise are not removed so quickly. This can lead to cramp and muscle soreness.

Cool down by doing very light exercise – brisk walking for example – to move the blood more quickly and get rid of the metabolic waste.

3 *Always get guidance on how to use weights correctly for strength training.*

4 *Build your programme at your own pace and make sure it suits you.* You need at least two sessions a week to work on your fitness and three is best. Enjoy the programme and change it regularly. There are many different activities you can do that will build your fitness; have a range available so you do not get bored. Fitness training is a means to an end – playing your sport. It has no extra health benefits, but train as if it mattered in itself. Exercise in a pleasant an environment as possible. It is easier to run in the park than by a busy road for example (and you won't get exhausted from the car fumes either).

5 *Don't rely on your sport to make you fit – get fit to play.*

6 *Exercise uses energy, which you must replace, so pay attention to your diet.* Sport is not divorced from the rest of your life; it is part of a healthy lifestyle with good eating habits.

7 *Keep a diary.* A diary is clear evidence of your commitment and progress. Writing anything down makes it more real and more important. Over the course of time it makes it easier for you to chart your progress and improvement.

8 *Exercise does not mean pain and injury.* Take care of yourself. Remember the saying 'No pain, no gain, insane'.

9 *Exercise regularly.* Half of the good effects of exercise are lost in six days, so if you exercise every two weeks, you will keep hardly any gains from your last session. Each session will be like starting from scratch.

These are only some of the main points in the vast subject of fitness and exercise. Mind and body work together and if you are fit and feel good about that, then you set up a virtuous circle where you feel confident, play well and feel even more confident. When you feel good, your mind will be sharp and focused and you will be able to use the mental skills in this book more effectively. Set up a sensible fitness programme and use your mental skills to motivate yourself to stick to it.

Eye Accessing Cues and Sensory-Based Words

Here are the most common eye movements, or eye accessing cues, that go with different ways of thinking. Most people tend to have this pattern. For some people it is reversed (i.e. remembered images and sounds are accessed on their right-hand side, feelings are accessed down to their left-hand side and self-talk is down to their right). Your eye accessing cues will be consistent whatever they are.

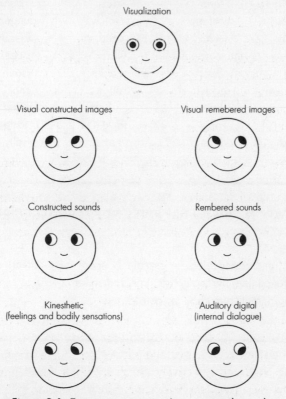

Visualization

Visual constructed images   Visual remebered images

Constructed sounds   Rembered sounds

Kinesthetic
(feelings and bodily sensations)   Auditory digital
(internal dialogue)

Figure 9.1: Eye accessing cues (as you see them when looking straight at another person)

PREDICATES — SENSORY-BASED LANGUAGE

Seeing	Hearing	Feeling	Smelling/Tasting
Visual	**Auditory**	**Kinesthetic**	**Olfactory/ Gustatory**
look	say	touch	scent
picture	question	move	smell
bright	accent	handle	fishy
focus	rhythm	contact	nosy
image	sing	grasp	fresh
colour	wavelength	smooth	smoky
insight	melody	push	fragrant
vivid	tone	rub	air
scene	resonate	scratch	pungent
blank	echo	solid	flavour
visualize	monotonous	warm	sweet
dark	deaf	cold	sour
perspective	speech	rough	choke
vision	tune	sensitive	bitter
shine	ring	tackle	taste
reflect	demand	turn	salty
eye	ask	push	juicy

Neutral words that do not imply any representational system

think, know, understand, decide, explain, conceptualize, attend, calculate, recognize, perceive, meditate, remember, evaluate, process, learn, motivate, change, consider

Visual Phrases

I see what you mean.
I have a hazy idea.
That is not very clear.
It appears this way.
The future looks bright.
It is a sight for sore eyes.

Olfactory and Gustatory Phrases

I smell a rat.
That's a fishy situation.
He has a taste for the good life.
She's a sweet person.
He made an acid comment.

Auditory Phrases

I'll turn a deaf ear.
That sounds good.
I hear what you are saying.
In a manner of speaking...
Repeat it word for word.

Kinesthetic Phrases

I will get in touch with you.
She's a cool competitor.
He was thick-skinned.
They had a heated argument.
He laid a firm foundation for
success.

Glossary

accessing cues	The ways we tune our bodies by our breathing, posture, gestures and eye movements to think in certain ways.
aerobic fitness (cardiovascular fitness)	The ability to take in, transport and use oxygen, leading to the cardiovascular system working more efficiently and a higher sustained metabolic rate and oxygen consumption in the muscles.
anchor	Any stimulus that evokes a response. Anchors change our *state*. They can occur naturally or be set up intentionally. They act as triggers to achieve a state.
anchoring	The process of associating one thing with another.
as if	Using the imagination to explore the consequences of thoughts or actions *as if* they had occurred. For example, when you behave *as if* you feel confident, those actions will start to make you feel more confident.
associated state	Being inside an experience, seeing through your own eyes, being fully in your senses.
attention	The light of consciousness that you can choose to shine on what you want to sense and understand.
auditory	To do with the sense of hearing.
balance	The ability to keep your equilibrium when moving.
baseline state	That *state* of mind which is normal and habitual for you.

behaviour	Any activity that we engage in, including thinking. Behaviour is one of the *neurological levels*.
beliefs	The *generalizations* we make about others, the world and ourselves that become our operating principles. We act *as if* they are true and they are true for us. Beliefs are one of the *neurological levels*.
beyond identity	That level of experience where you are most yourself and most your Self and you are most connected with others. One of the *neurological levels*. Often called 'vision' or 'the spiritual level'.
body language	The way we communicate with our body, without words or sounds – for example, our posture, gestures, facial expressions, appearance and eye movements.
break state	Using any movement or *distraction* to change an emotional *state*. A deep breath can be a break state. A neutral *anchor* can be used as a break state when you are upset during a game.
calibration	Accurately recognizing your own or another person's *state* by reading non-verbal signals.
capability	A successful *strategy* for carrying out a task; a skill or habit; also a habitual way of thinking. One of the *neurological levels*.
cardiovascular	To do with the heart and circulatory system.
cardiovascular fitness	*See aerobic fitness.*
chunking	Changing your perception by going up or down a level.
concentration	The degree to which you are capable of focusing your *attention* and ignoring *distractions*.
congruence	The alignment of *beliefs*, *values*, skills and action, so that you 'walk your talk'. Congruence also means being in *rapport* with oneself and is the opposite of self-sabotage.

conscious	Anything in present moment awareness.
context	The particular setting such as time, place and people that gives a particular meaning to events. Certain actions are possible in one context (e.g. a boxing match), that are not allowed in other contexts (e.g. a public street).
contrastive analysis	Comparing two or more elements and looking for critical differences between them in order to understand them better.
cool down	Light exercise after the main exercise to help the muscles recover and bring the heart rate and blood pressure back to normal.
critical submodalities	Those *submodalities* that make an important difference to your experience if you change them.
delayed muscle soreness	Muscle soreness that starts a day or two after unfamiliar or unusually vigorous exercise. You are likely to feel it after the first match of the season.
deletion	Missing out a portion of an experience.
dissociated state	Being at one remove from an experience, seeing or hearing it as if from the outside, somehow feeling 'out of it' or 'spacy'.
distortion	Changing experience, making it different in some way.
distraction	When your *attention* is somewhere other than where you want it to be.
downtime	In a light *trance* with your *attention* inwards on your own *state*.
drone zone	Where you feel insufficiently challenged and lacking in energy and intensity.
ecology	A concern and exploration of the overall consequences of your thoughts and actions on the total web of relationships in which you are part. There is also 'internal ecology', how a person's different thoughts and feelings fit together so they are *congruent* or *incongruent*.

elicitation	Drawing out or evoking some *behaviour*, *state* or *strategy*.
emotional state	*See state.*
environment	The where, the when and the people we are with. One of the *neurological levels*.
first position	Perceiving the world from your own point of view only. Being in touch with your own inner reality. One of three different *perceptual positions*, the others being *second* and *third position*.
fitness	The ability of your body to perform work – a mixture of aerobic capacity and muscular *strength*, endurance, *suppleness* and *speed* that enhances your health, mood, quality of life and sporting success.
flow state	Where everything is easy and effortless. *See also The zone.*
focus	*See concentration.*
frame	Way of looking at something, a particular point of view, e.g. *goal* frame looks at what you do in relation to your goals.
future pace	To *mentally rehearse* a *goal*. A mental simulation of hoped-for future events.
generalization	The process by which one specific experience comes to represent a whole class or group of experiences.
goal	Something you want, a *state*, achievement or prize that you are prepared to work for.
gustatory	To do with the sense of taste.
health	The natural state of *balance* and well-being in the mind, body and spirit.
identity	Your self-image or self-concept. Who you take yourself to be. One of the *neurological levels*.
imagery	Using your senses mentally – seeing, hearing, feeling in your imagination in order to

	mentally *rehearse* or prepare for a game or event.
incongruence	A *state* of being out of *rapport* with oneself, having internal conflict expressed in *behaviour*. It may be sequential – for example, one action followed by another that contradicts it – or simultaneous – for example, agreement in words but with a doubtful voice tone.
intensity	The level of physical or mental exertion.
internal dialogue	Talking to oneself.
kinesthetic	The feeling sense, tactile sensations and internal feelings such as remembered sensations, emotions and the sense of *balance*.
map of reality (model of the world)	Each person's unique representation of the world built from their individual perceptions and experiences. It is not simply a concept but a whole way of living, breathing and acting.
matching	Adopting parts of another person's *behaviour*, skills, *belief* or *values*.
mental rehearsal	Mentally playing through your sporting *goals* using *imagery* to prepare yourself and build technical skill.
metabolism	The processes of the body that produce and use energy.
metaphor	Indirect communication by a story or figure of speech implying a comparison. In NLP metaphor covers similes, stories, parables and allegories. Metaphor implies overtly or covertly that one thing is like another.
modelling	The process of discerning the sequence of ideas and *behaviour* that enable someone to accomplish a task. The basis of *neuro-linguistic programming*.

neuro-linguistic programming	The study of excellence and the study of the structure of subjective experience.
neurological levels	Different levels of experience: *environment, behaviour, capability, belief, identity* and *beyond identity*, developed mainly by Robert Dilts.
olfactory	To do with the sense of smell.
outcome	A specific sensory-based desired *goal*.
overtraining	Excess exercise, either too frequent or of too great intensity (or both), that leads to illness, injury and lack of energy.
pacing	Gaining and maintaining *rapport* with another person over a period of time by meeting them in their *model of the world*. Pacing yourself is paying *attention* to your own experience without immediately trying to change it.
perceptual position	The viewpoint we take, either *first position* (our own), *second position* (another person's) or *third position* (the relationship between the two).
positive intention	The positive purpose underlying any action or *belief*.
preferred representational system	The *representational system* that an individual typically uses most to think consciously and organize their experience. It will come out particularly when the person is under stress.
presuppositions	Ideas or *beliefs* that are presupposed, i.e. taken for granted and acted upon.
rapport	A relationship of trust and responsiveness with self or others.
representational systems	Ways of thinking. The different channels whereby we re-present information on the inside, using our senses: visual (sight), *auditory* (hearing), *kinesthetic* (body sensation), *olfactory* (smell) and *gustatory* (taste).

resources	Anything that can help one achieve an *outcome*, e.g. physiology, *states*, thoughts, *beliefs*, *strategies*, experiences, people, events, possessions, places, stories, etc.
second position	Experiencing the point of view of another person.
self-modelling	Modelling your own states of excellence as resources.
sensory acuity	The process of learning to make finer and more useful distinctions from the sensory information we get from the world.
speed	The time from stimulus to response – your reaction time, the time to complete the movement needed in your sport. An important part of overall *fitness*.
spiritual	*See Beyond identity*.
stamina	The ability to persist over long periods and avoid tiredness and fatigue.
state	The sum of our thoughts, feelings, emotions, physical and mental energy.
strategy	A repeatable sequence of thoughts leading to actions that consistently produce a particular goal.
strength	The ability of muscles to exert force.
submodalities	The fine distinctions we make within each *representational system*, the qualities of our internal representations, the smallest building blocks of our thoughts.
suppleness	The range of movement you are capable of, the degree of stretch and flexibility of your body.
tension	The degree of muscle contraction. When used psychologically it means the degree to which you feel stressed because the challenges you face seem to be greater than the *resources* you have to cope with them. Physical and psychological tension usually go together.

third position	Taking the viewpoint of a detached observer, the systemic view.
training zone	The heart rate level to aim for during aerobic exercise. Defined as between 70 per cent and 80 per cent of the figure you obtain after taking your age from 220.
trance	An altered *state* resulting in a temporarily fixed, narrowed and inward focus of *attention*.
unconscious	Everything that is not in your present moment awareness.
uptime	In a *state* with your *attention* outwards.
values	Those things, like health, that are important to you.
vestibular system	The sense of *balance*.
warm up	Light exercise prior to the main training exercise to stretch muscles, prepare the body and avoid the risk of injury.
weight training	Exercising using weights to provide resistance to the muscles. Essential to develop *strength*.
the zone	The *state* where you play above your best and everything seems effortless.

Bibliography

American College of Sports Medicine, *Position statement on the recommended quantity and quality of exercise for developing and maintaining cardiorespiratory and muscular fitness in healthy adults*, 1990

Bandura, A., *Social Foundations of Thought and Action*, Prentice-Hall, 1986

Bull, S., Albinson, J., and Shambrook, C., *The Mental Game Plan*, Sports Dynamics, 1996

Butler, R., *Sports Psychology in Action*, Heinemann, 1996

Csikszentmihalyi, M., *Flow*, Rider, 1992

Cunningham, L., *Hypnosport*, Westwood, 1981

Gallwey, T., *The Inner Game of Golf*, Pan, 1986

--, *The Inner Game of Tennis*, Pan, 1986

Garratt, E., *Sporting Excellence*, Crown House, 1999

Harris, D., and Harris, B., *The Athlete's Guide to Sports Psychology: Mental Training for Physical People*, Leisure Press, 1984

Health Education Authority and Sports Council, *Allied Dunbar National Fitness Survey*, Sports Council and HEA, 1992

Hemery, D., *et al.*, *Winning without Drugs*, Thorsons, 1990

Horn, T. (ed.), *Advances in Sport Psychology*, Human Kinetics, 1992

Loehr, J., *The New Toughness Training for Sports*, Plume, 1995

Mackenzie, M., *Golf: The Mind Game*, Dell, 1990

--, *Tennis: The Mind Game*, Dell, 1991

McLatchie, G., *Essentials of Sports Medicine*, Churchill Livingstone, 1990

Martens, R., *Coaches' Guide to Sports Psychology*, Human Kinetics, 1987

Morgan, W., *Forty Years of Progress Sports Psychology in Exercise and Sports Medicine*, American College of Sports Medicine, 1994

O'Connor, J., and Seymour, J., *Introducing NLP*, Thorsons, 1994

O'Connor, J., and McDermott, I., *NLP and Health*, Thorsons, 1996

Orlick, T., *In Pursuit of Excellence*, Leisure Press, 1990

--, *Psyching for Sport: Mental Training for Athletes*, Leisure Press, 1986

Pargman, D. (ed.), *Psychological Basis of Sport Injuries*, Fitness Information Technology, 1993

Roberts, G. (ed.), *Motivation in Sport and Exercise*, Human Kinetics, 1992

Sharkey, B., *The Physiology of Fitness*, Human Kinetics, 1990

Singer, R., Murhey, M., and Tennant, L., *Handbook of Research on Sports Psychology*, Macmillan, 1993

Straub, W., and Williams, J. (eds), *Cognitive Sport Psychology*, Sport Science Associates, 1984

Syer, J., and Connolly, C., *Sporting Body, Sporting Mind*, Simon & Schuster, 1984

Taylor, J., *The Mental Edge for Competitive Sports*, Minuteman, 1993

Tutko, T., and Tosi, U., *Sports Psyching*, Tarcher, 1976

Unestal, L-E., *New Paths of Sport Learning and Excellence*, Orebro University, Sweden, 1981

Ungerleider, S., *Mental Training for Peak Performance*, Rodale, 1996

Vernacchia, R., McGuire R., and Cook, D., *Coaching Mental Excellence*, Warde Publishers, 1996

Williams, J. (ed.), *Applied Sports Psychology: Personal Growth to Peak Performance*, Mayfield, 1993

Training and Resources

Audiotapes, NLP training and consultancy

Many of these exercises are available on audiotape, including the unconscious process, mental rehearsal though imagery and accelerated healing patterns. For details of audiotapes and also information about NLP training and consultancy contact:

Lambent Training
4 Coombe Gardens
New Malden
Surrey
KT3 4AA
Tel: 020 8715 2560
Fax: 020 8715 2560
e-mail: lambent@well.com

For sports mental training and consultancy

The Sports Performance Institute
Littlebrook House
The Brownings
Box
Corsham
Wiltshire
SN13 8HP
e-fax: 0870 127 2320
e-mail: cobden@cwcom.net

For sports psychology information and accreditation courses

The National Coaching Foundation
114 Cardigan Road
Headingly
Leeds LS6 3BJ
Tel: 0113 274 4802

The Sports Council
16 Upper Woburn Place
London WC1H 0QP
Tel: 020 7388 1277

The British Olympic Association
1 Wandsworth Plain
London SW18 1EH
Tel: 020 8871 2677

For information on sport medicine

The National Sports Medicine Institute
Medical College, St Bartholomew's
Charterhouse Square
London EC1M 6BQ
Tel: 020 7251 0583

Index of Exercises

Chapter 3

Exercise 10: Preparing Imagery – Pictures

Page 61
Purpose   To practise visualization for mental rehearsal.
Problem   Being unable to make clear, controllable pictures.
Benefit   A growing ability to visualize clearly.

Exercise 11: Preparing Imagery – Associated and Dissociated

Page 63
Purpose   To practise associating and dissociating.
Problem   Being unsure of which perspective to use.
Benefit   The ability to use the right perspective for your imagery.

Exercise 12: Preparing Imagery – Sounds

Page 65
Purpose   To practise hearing sounds mentally for mental rehearsal.
Problem   Having difficulty in getting clear, controllable sounds.
Benefit   The ability to hear sounds mentally to enhance the imagery practice.

Exercise 13: Preparing Imagery – Feelings, Tastes and Smells

Page 65
Purpose   To practise getting feelings for mental rehearsal.
Problem   Having difficulty with clear, controllable feelings attached to the imagery.
Benefit   The ability to use strong feelings in imagery practice.

Exercise 14: Discovering your Preferred Way of Thinking

Page 67
Purpose   To know your own way of thinking in order to design the best way to employ imagery.
Problem   Being unsure about your preferred way of thinking.
Benefit   Knowing how you think so you can make your imagery more effective.

Exercise 15: Finding your Critical Submodalities for Mental Rehearsal

Page 69

Purpose   To find the exact qualities of thought needed for the most
              effective mental rehearsal.

Problem   Being uncertain exactly how to use mental rehearsal.

Benefit   To provide a made-to-measure imagery practice schedule.

Exercise 16: Using Imagery to Improve your Skills

Page 75

Purpose   To improve your sporting skills.

Problem   The need for technical practice.

Benefit   More technical skill — no sweat!

Exercise 17: A Record Leap of the Imagination

Page 81

Purpose   To get to know what your opponent is thinking.

Problem   Finding coaching difficult or not being able to anticipate
              your opponent's game.

Benefit   Being able to anticipate your opponent's game; better
              coaching skills.

Exercise 18: Performer, Coach, Referee

Page 82

Purpose   To prepare comprehensively for an event.

Problem   Lack of preparation.

Benefit   Confidence that the venue will not distract you from your
              game.

Chapter 4

Exercise 19: Critical Concentration Points

Page 95

Purpose   To identify the points where you need to concentrate and
              how to do it.

Problem   Concentration lapses at important points in the game.

Benefit   Staying focused at critical points of the game.

Benefit   One way into the zone; more time to play shots and see the ball; your opponents seem to be moving more slowly than usual.

Chapter 6

Exercise 30: Balancing your Breathing

Page 145

Purpose   To balance your energy level.

Problem   No particular problem – this exercise gives a good anchor to break out of strong negative feelings or a feeling of over-intensity.

Benefit   Feeling more energized and balanced.

Exercise 31: Dealing with Anxiety before the Game

Page 147

Purpose   To stop feeling anxious.

Problem   Overstimulation and unpleasant anxious feelings before the game.

Benefit   Better concentration, more confidence.

Exercise 32: Awareness

Page 153

Purpose   To gain relaxation and emotional balance.

Problem   No particular problem.

Benefit   Being able to gather your resources and relax and balance your energy.

Chapter 7

Exercise 33: Mistakes to Insight

Page 160

Purpose   To analyse mistakes after the match and use them to improve your future play.

Problem   Making the same mistake consistently in your game.

Benefit   Being able to eliminate mistakes and play better.

Exercise 34: Enjoying your Sport

Page 163
Purpose   To make the most of the times when you played well and enjoyed playing.
Problem   Not noticing when you play well or feeling 'stale'.
Benefit   Feeling enthusiastic and motivated.

Exercise 35: Accelerating Healing

Page 167
Purpose   To heal quickly and easily.
Problem   Sports injury.
Benefit   Healing.

Exercise 36: Review

Page 172
Purpose   To align and model your best resources.
Problem   Feeling 'disconnected' from your resources and skills.
Benefit   Reconnecting with your resources and skills.

EXERCISE FINDER

Problem

Achieving your best play

Anxiety before the match

Concentration lapses

Dealing with anger and outbursts of emotion

Feeling rushed or hurried, not enough time in game

Fitness

Goal setting

Lack of confidence

Lack of enjoyment

Lack of ideas for coaching

Lack of motivation

About the Author

Joseph O'Connor is the author of 12 books on NLP, communication skills and systemic thinking. He works internationally as a trainer and consultant for business. He also works with athletes, using NLP to enhance their mental training and preparation, and has modelled excellent tennis coaching skills. He plays squash and enjoys it thoroughly. Joseph is co-founder of the Sports Performance Institute, which offers mental training and consultancy for athletes and teams in every sport. For more information contact:

The Sports Performance Institute
Littlebrook House
The Brownings
Box
Corsham
Wiltshire
SN13 8HP
e-fax: 0870 127 2320
e-mail: cobden@cwcom.net

To find out more about NLP training and consultancy contact:

Lambent Training
4 Coombe Gardens
New Malden
Surrey
KT3 4AA
Tel: 020 8715 2560
Fax: 020 8715 2560
e-mail: lambent@well.com
website: www.lambent.com

Lambent Training also offers other NLP training and short courses. Call or write for details.

Other books by Joseph O'Connor:

The Art of Systems Thinking (with Ian McDermott)
Extraordinary Solutions for Everyday Problems
Introducing NLP (with John Seymour)
Leading with NLP
NLP and Health (with Ian McDermott)
NLP and Relationships (with Robin Prior)
Not Pulling Strings
Practical NLP for Managers (with Ian McDermott)
Principles of NLP (with Ian McDermott)
Successful Selling with NLP (with Robin Prior)
Training with NLP (with John Seymour)

Index

Index of Athletes